Crochet Blocks

60 Easy-To-Make Motifs & 15 Stunning Projects

Agnieszka Strycharska

F - treble crochet
o chain
x single crochet
double

Tuva Publishing

www.tuvapublishing.com

Address Merkez Mah. Cavusbasi Cad. No:71
Cekmekoy - Istanbul 34782 / Turkey
Tel: +9 0216 642 62 62

Crochet Blocks

First Print 2016 / April

All Global Copyrights Belong To
Tuva Tekstil ve Yayıncılık Ltd.

Content Crochet Patterns

Editor in Chief Ayhan DEMİRPEHLİVAN
Project Editor Kader DEMİRPEHLİVAN
Designer Agnieszka STRYCHARSKA
Technical Editors Wendi CUSINS, Leyla ARAS, Büşra ESER
Graphic Designers Ömer ALP, Abdullah BAYRAKÇI
Assistant Zilal ÖNEL
Photograph Tuva Publishing, Agnieszka STRYCHARSKA

ISBN 978-605-9192-14-9

Printing House
Bilnet Matbaacılık ve Ambalaj San. A.Ş.

TuvaYayincilik TuvaPublishing
TuvaYayincilik TuvaPublishing

Contents

Preface

Like most crochet enthusiasts, the first crochet motif I ever made was a simple granny square. It is still one of my favorite motifs and I often use them in my projects. These days I enjoy the challenge of more complicated motifs.

I love incorporating crochet motifs into my designs, as they are never boring. They are so versatile and can be used in so many different ways. Whether I'm making a hat, a bag, a scarf or even a skirt, motifs bring me great joy while crocheting them.

Colors are amazing to use when making motifs. The variety of shades available stimulates my creativity. Often I find myself making the same motif using a different color scheme and then coming up with a whole new design or discovering a new use for it. I find that using only one color can also be very effective – giving a more modern, elegant look to the project.

For this book, I have chosen to share my favorite motifs – from simple designs to those which are a little more challenging. To inspire you even more, I've included projects which use some of these motifs.

I dedicate this book to my daughters, Sophie and Mary, with all my love. It is my hope that this book will nurture their skills and passion for crochet, so that one day they will love crochet as much as I do.

Agnieszka Strycharska

Motif Gallery

6.

7.

9.

8.

10.

16.

19.

17.

18.

20.

26.

27.

28.

29.

30.

31.

33.

32.

35.

34.

14

36.

37.

39.

38.

40.

15

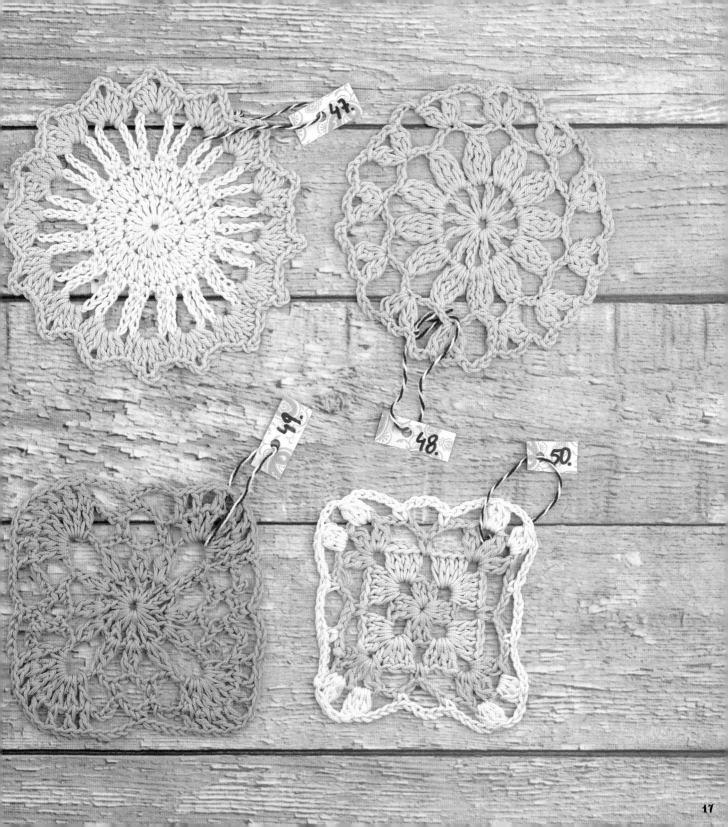

59.

56.

60.

58.

57.

20

Hat - Page 106 · Cowl - Page 116

Motifs

Motif 1

PATTERN

Base Round: Using Color A, ch 4; join with sl st to first ch to form a ring.

ROUND 1: (Right Side) Ch 1 (NOT counted as first st), 8 sc in ring; join with sl st to first sc. (8 sc).

ROUND 2: Ch 3 (counts as first dc, now and throughout), [yo, insert hook in same st as joining, pull up lp, yo, draw through 2 lps on hook] 3 times (4 lps on hook), yo, draw through all 4 lps (first 4-bob made), ch 2; [4-bob in next sc, ch 2] around; join with sl st to first dc (3rd ch of beginning ch-3). Fasten off Color A and weave in all ends. (8 bobbles & 8 ch-2 sps).

ROUND 3: With right side facing, join Color B with sl st to any first ch-2 sp, ch 3, 2 dc in same sp, ch 1, (3-bob, ch 3, 3-bob) in next ch-2 sp, ch 1, *3 dc in next ch-2 sp, ch 1, (3-bob, ch 3, 3-bob) in next ch-2 sp, ch 1; rep from * around; join with sl st to first dc. Fasten off Color B and weave in all ends. (8 bobbles, 12 dc, 8 ch-1 sps & 4 ch-3 sps).

Materials
Hook: H-8 (5.00 mm)

DMC Natura XL:
Color A - 73 Light Grey
Color B - 82 Yellow

Finished Size: 4¼" (11 cm)

3-Bobble Stitch (3-bob): Yo, insert hook into st or sp indicated, pull up lp, yo, draw through 2 lps on hook, [yo, insert hook in same st or sp, pull up lp, yo, draw through 2 lps on hook] 2 times more (4 lps on hook), yo and draw through all 4 lps.

4-Bobble Stitch (4-bob): Yo, insert hook into st or sp indicated, pull up lp, yo, draw through 2 lps on hook, [yo, insert hook in same st or sp, pull up lp, yo, draw through 2 lps on hook] 3 times more (5 lps on hook), yo and draw through all 5 lps.

Note: The first Bobble Stitch in a round is started differently to subsequent bobbles in round. Instructions for the first bobble are included within the pattern. For subsequent bobbles follow the directions above.

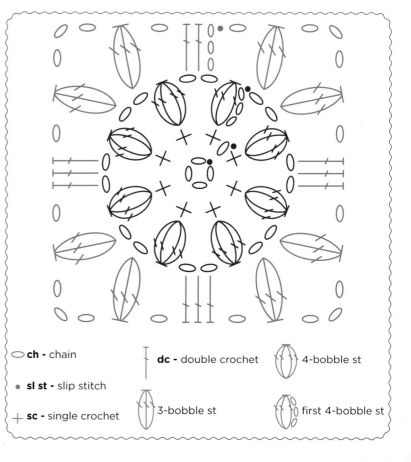

◯ **ch -** chain

● **sl st -** slip stitch

╋ **sc -** single crochet

dc - double crochet

3-bobble st

4-bobble st

first 4-bobble st

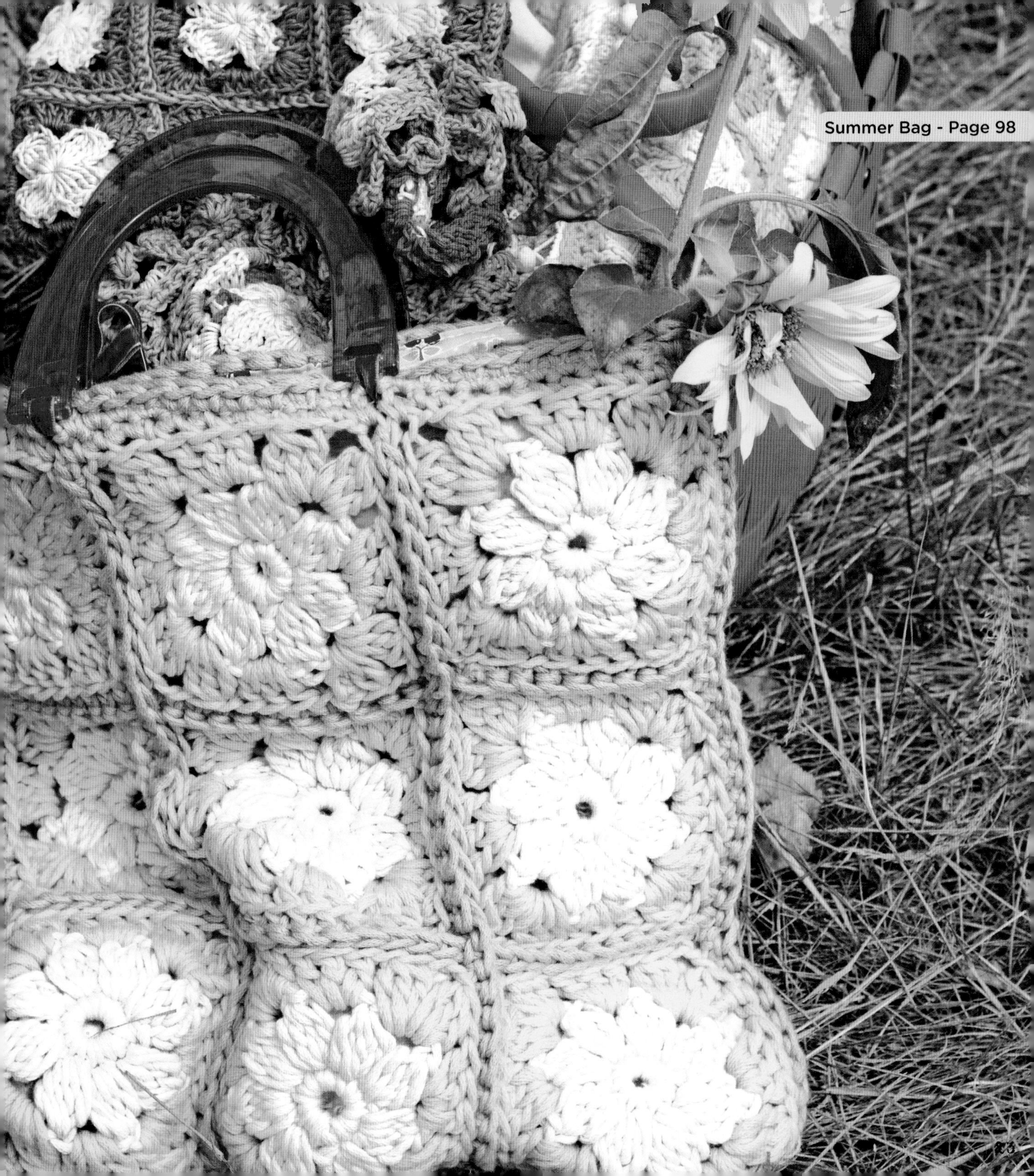

Summer Bag - Page 98

Motif 2

Materials
Hook: E-4 (3.50 mm)

DMC Natura Just Cotton:
Color A – N 51 Erica
Color B – N 85 Giroflée
Color C – N 74 Curry

Finished Size: 2¾" (7 cm)

4-Bobble Stitch (4-bob): Yo, insert hook into st or sp indicated, pull up lp, yo, draw through 2 lps on hook, [yo, insert hook in same st or sp, pull up lp, yo, draw through 2 lps on hook] 3 times more (5 lps on hook), yo and draw through all 5 lps.

Note: The first Bobble Stitch in a round is started differently to subsequent bobbles in round. Instructions for the first bobble are included within the pattern. For subsequent bobbles follow the directions above.

PATTERN

Base Round: Using Color A, ch 4; join with sl st to first ch to form a ring.

ROUND 1: (Right Side) Ch 3 (counts as first dc, now and throughout), 15 dc in ring; join with sl st to first dc (3rd ch of beginning ch-3). (16 dc) Fasten off Color A and weave in all ends.

ROUND 2: With right side facing, join Color B with sl st to same st as joining, ch 1 (NOT counted as first st), sc in same st, ch 1, skip next dc, 7 dc in next dc, ch 1, skip next dc, *sc in next dc, ch 1, skip next dc, 7 dc in next dc, ch 1, skip next dc; rep from * around; join with sl st to first sc. (28 dc, 4 sc & 8 ch-1 sps) Fasten off Color B and weave in all ends.

ROUND 3: With right side facing, join Color C with sl st to last ch-1 sp on Round 2, ch 3, [yo, insert hook in same st as joining, pull up lp, yo, draw through 2 lps on hook] 3 times (4 lps on hook), yo, draw through all 4 lps (first 4-bob made), ch 2, 4-bob in next ch-1 sp, ch 2, skip next 3 dc, sc in next dc (center dc of 7-dc group), ch 2, skip next 3 dc, *[4-bob in next ch-1 sp, ch 2] 2 times, sc in center dc of next 7-dc group, ch 2; rep from * around; join with sl st to first dc. (8 bobbles, 4 sc & 12 ch-2 sps) Fasten off Color C and weave in all ends.

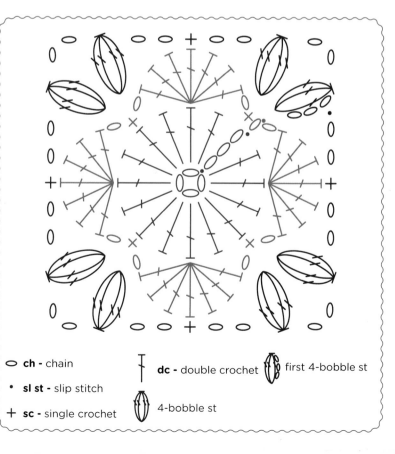

ch - chain

sl st - slip stitch

sc - single crochet

dc - double crochet

first 4-bobble st

4-bobble st

Skirt - Page 102

25

Motif 3

PATTERN

Base Round: Using Color A, ch 4; join with sl st to first ch to form a ring.
ROUND 1: (Right Side) Ch 1 (NOT counted as first st), *sc in ring, ch 4, 4tr-bob in ring, ch 4; rep from * 3 times more; join with sl st to first sc. (4 bobbles, 4 sc & 8 ch-4 lps) Fasten off Color A and weave in all ends.
ROUND 2: With right side facing, using Color B, join with sc to 2nd ch of second ch-4 lp (after first bobble), ch 5, skip next 2 ch, skip next sc, on next ch-4 lp, skip next 2 ch, sc in next (3rd) ch, ch 3, skip next ch, skip next bobble, *on next ch-4 lp, sc in 2nd ch, ch 5, on next ch-4 lp, sc in 3rd ch, ch 3; rep from * around; join with sl st to first sc. (8 sc, 4 ch-5 lps & 4 ch-3 lps)
ROUND 3: Sl st in first ch-5 lp, ch 3 (counts as first dc), (2 dc, ch 1, 3 dc) in same lp, ch 1, 3 dc in next ch-3 lp, ch 1, *(3 dc, ch 1, 3 dc) in next ch-5 lp, ch 1, 3 dc in next ch-3 lp, ch 1; rep from * around; join with sl st to first dc (3rd ch of beg ch-3). (36 dc & 12 ch-1 sps) Fasten off Color B and weave in all ends.

Materials
Hook: E-4 (3.50 mm)

DMC Natura Just Cotton:
Color A – N 43 Golden Lemon
Color B – N 26 Blue Jeans

Finished Size: 2¾" (7 cm)

4-Treble Bobble (4tr-bob): Wrap yarn twice around hook, insert hook into st or sp indicated, pull up lp (4 lps on hook), [yo, draw through 2 lps on hook] 2 times (2 lps on hook), *wrap yarn twice around hook, insert hook in same st or sp, pull up lp, [yo, draw through 2 lps on hook] 2 times, rep from * 2 times more (5 lps on hook), yo and draw through all 5 lps.

Join with Single Crochet: With slip knot on hook, insert hook in st or sp indicated, pull up lp (2 lps on hook), yo, draw through both loops on hook (first single crochet made).

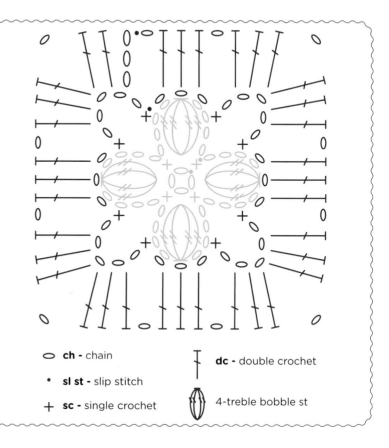

○ **ch -** chain

• **sl st -** slip stitch

+ **sc -** single crochet

┬ **dc -** double crochet

4-treble bobble st

Motif 4

PATTERN

Base Round: Using Color A, ch 4; join with sl st to first ch to form a ring.

ROUND 1: (Right Side) Ch 5 (counts as first dc and ch-2), [dc in ring, ch 2] 7 times; join with sl st to first dc (3rd ch of beg ch-5). (8 dc & 8 ch-2 sps)

ROUND 2: Sl st in next ch-2 sp, ch 2 (counts as first hdc), (3 dc, hdc) in same sp, *(hdc, 3 dc, hdc) in next ch-2 sp; rep from * around; join with sl st to first hdc (2nd ch of beg ch-2).

ROUND 3: Ch 8 (counts as first dc and ch-5), skip next 3 dc, dc in sp between next 2 hdc, ch 7, skip next 3 dc, *dc in sp between next 2 hdc, ch 5, skip next 3 dc, dc in sp between next 2 hdc, ch 7, skip next 3 dc; rep from * around; join with sl st to first dc (3rd ch of beg ch-8). (8 dc, 4 ch-5 lps & 4 ch-7 lps)

ROUND 4: Sl st in next ch-5 lp, ch 3 (counts as first dc), 3 dc in same lp, ch 1, (3 dc, ch 1, 3 dc) in next ch-7 lp, ch 1, *4 dc in next ch-5 lp, ch 1, (3 dc, ch 1, 3 dc) in next ch-7 lp, ch 1; rep from * around; join with sl st to first dc (3rd ch of beg ch-3). (40 dc & 12 ch-1 sps) Fasten off and weave in all ends.

Materials
Hook: J-10 (6.00 mm)

DMC Natura Just Cotton:
Color A – N 46 Forêt

Finished Size: 3½" (9 cm)

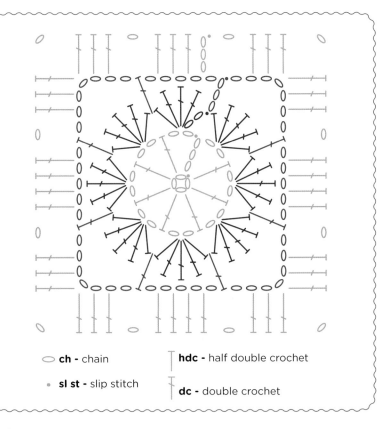

○ **ch** - chain

• **sl st** - slip stitch

† **hdc** - half double crochet

† **dc** - double crochet

Rug - Page 108

Motif 5

PATTERN

Base Round: Using Color A, ch 4; join with sl st to first ch to form a ring.

ROUND 1: (Right Side) Ch 1 (NOT counted as first st, now and throughout), 12 sc in ring; join with sl st to first sc. (12 sc)

ROUND 2: Ch 11, sl st in same st as joining, *(sl st, ch 11, sl st) in next sc; rep from * around. Fasten off Color A and weave in all ends.

ROUND 3: With right side facing, join Color B with sl st to any ch-11 lp (at top of petal), ch 1, sc in same lp, ch 2, sc in top of next ch-11 lp, ch 2, (3 dc, ch 1, 3 dc) in next ch-11 lp, ch 2, *[sc in top of next lp, ch 2] 2 times, (3 dc, ch 1, 3 dc) in next lp, ch 2; rep from * around; join with sl st to first sc. Fasten off Color B and weave in all ends.

Materials
Hook: E-4 (3.50 mm)

DMC Natura Just Cotton:
Color A – N 06 Rose Layette
Color B – N 38 Liquen

Finished Size: 2¾" (7 cm)

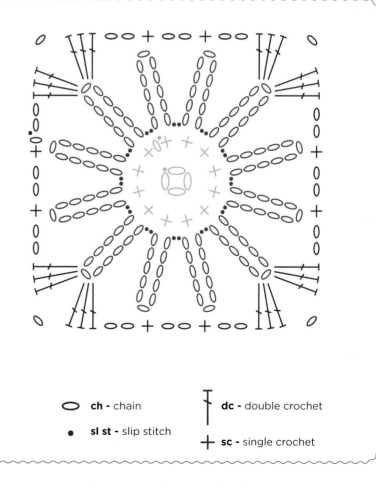

○ **ch** - chain

● **sl st** - slip stitch

┼ **dc** - double crochet

+ **sc** - single crochet

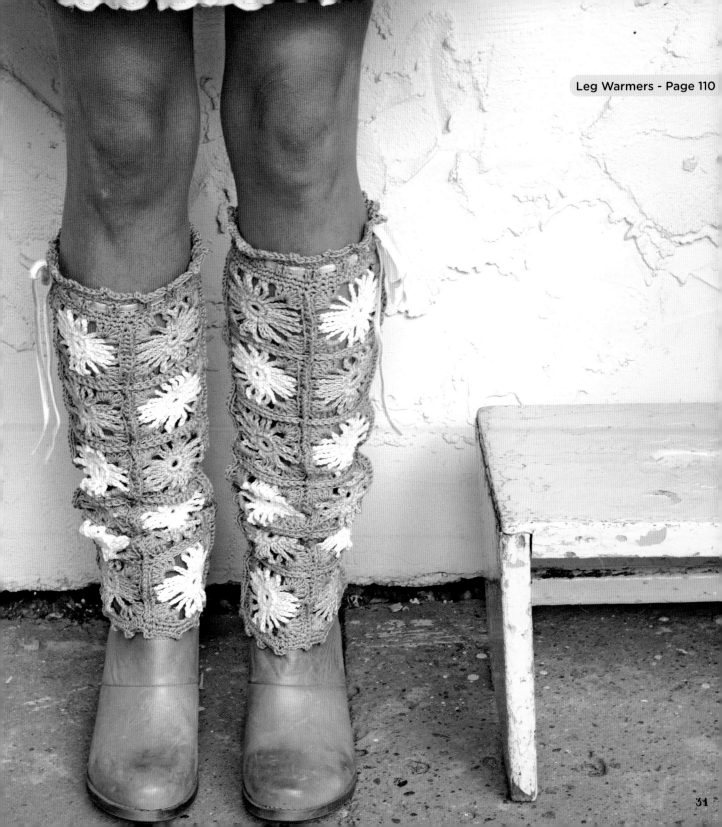

Motif 6

PATTERN

Base Round: Using Color A, ch 4; join with sl st to first ch to form a ring.

ROUND 1: (Right Side) Ch 3 (counts as first dc), yo, insert hook in ring, pull up lp, yo, draw through 2 lps on hook (2 lps on hook), yo and draw through all lps (first 2-bob made), ch 2, [2-bob in ring, ch 2] 7 times; join with sl st to first dc (3rd ch of beg ch-3). (8 bobbles & 8 ch-2 sps).

ROUND 2: Sl st in first ch-2 sp, ch 2 (counts as first hdc), (3 dc, hdc) in same sp, *(hdc, 3 dc, hdc) in next ch-2 sp; rep from * around; join with sl st to first hdc (2nd ch of beg ch-2). (8 petals) Fasten off and weave in all ends.

ROUND 3: With right side facing, working behind petals (bend them forward out of the way), using Color A, join with sc to top of any bobble in Round 1, ch 5, sc in next bobble, ch 3, *sc in next bobble, ch 5, sc in next bobble, ch 3; rep from * around; join with sl st to first sc. (8 sc, 4 ch-3 lps & 4 ch-5 lps)

ROUND 4: Sl st in first ch-5 lp, ch 1, (NOT counted as first st), (sc, hdc, dc, ch 1, dc, hdc, sc) in same lp, ch 1, 3 sc in next ch-3 lp, ch 1, *(sc, hdc, dc, ch 1, dc, hdc, sc) in next ch-5 lp, ch 1, 3 sc in next ch-3 lp, ch 1; rep from * around; join with sl st to first sc. Fasten off and weave in all ends.

Materials
Hook: E-4 (3.50 mm)

DMC Natura Just Cotton:
Color A – N 38 Liquen

Finished Size: 2¼" (6 cm)

2-Bobble Stitch (2-bob): Yo, insert hook into st or sp indicated, pull up lp, yo, draw through 2 lps on hook, yo, insert hook in same st or sp, pull up lp, yo, draw through 2 lps on hook (3 lps on hook), yo and draw through all 3 lps.

Note: The first Bobble Stitch in a round is started differently to subsequent bobbles in round. Instructions for the first bobble are included within the pattern. For subsequent bobbles follow the instructions above.

Join with Single Crochet: With slip knot on hook, insert hook in st or sp indicated, pull up lp (2 lps on hook), yo, draw through both loops on hook (first single crochet made).

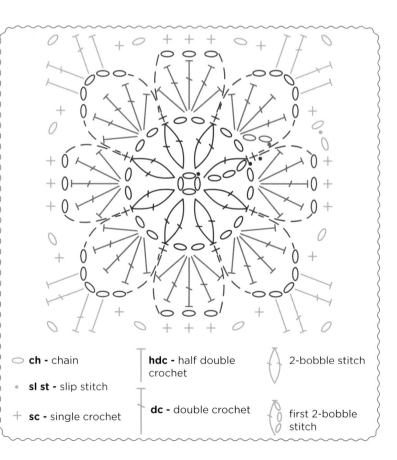

⬯ **ch** - chain	**hdc** - half double crochet	**2-bobble stitch**
• **sl st** - slip stitch		
+ **sc** - single crochet	**dc** - double crochet	**first 2-bobble stitch**

Small Purse - Page 112

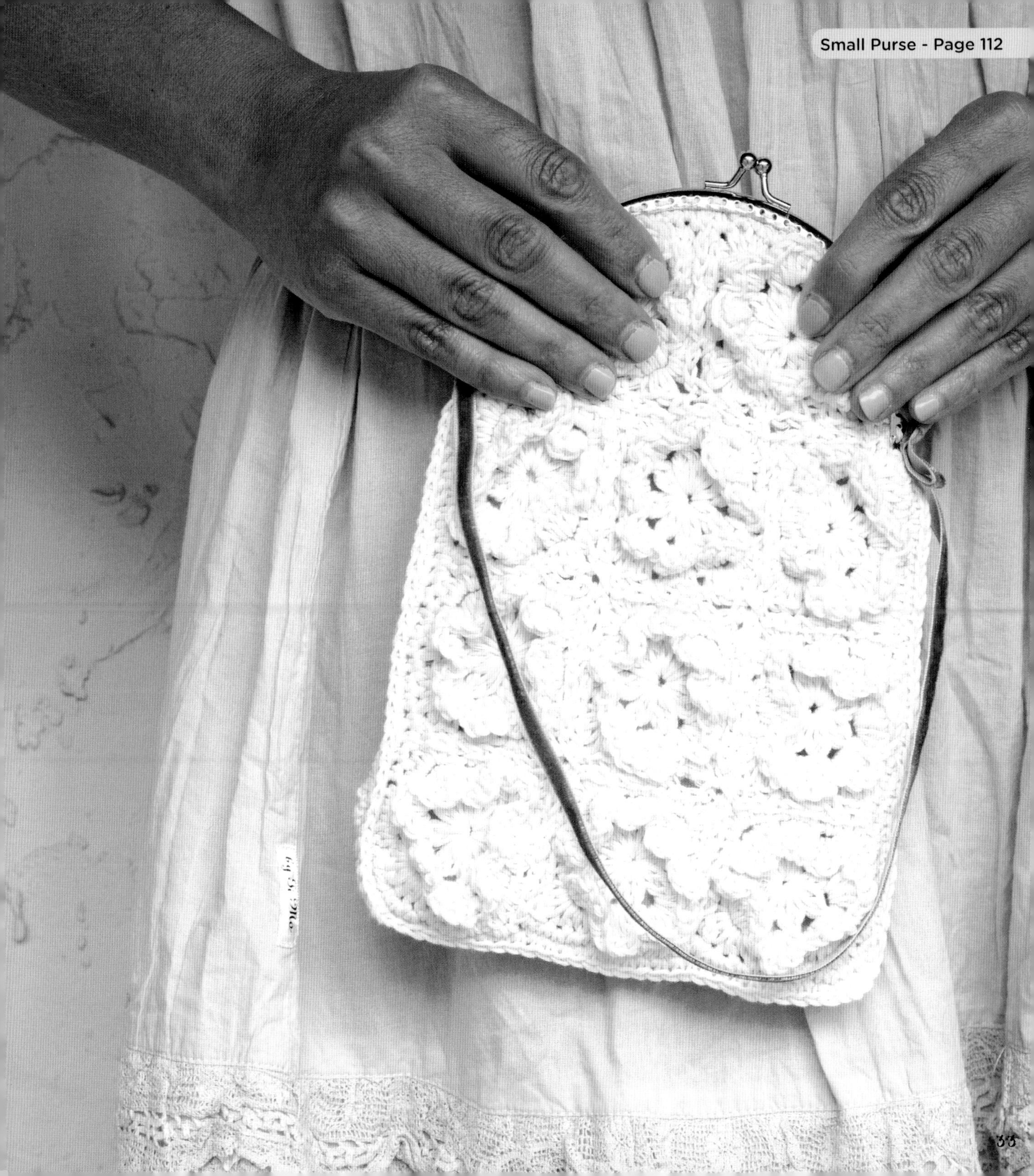

PATTERN

Base Round: Using Color A, ch 4; join with sl st to first ch to form a ring.

ROUND 1: (Right Side) Ch 4 (counts as first dc and ch-1), [dc in ring, ch 1] 11 times; join with sl st to first dc (3rd ch of beg ch-4). (12 dc & 12 ch-1 sps) Fasten off Color A and weave in all ends.

ROUND 2: With right side facing, join Color B with sl st in first ch-1 sp, ch 4 (counts as first hdc & ch-2), hdc in same sp, [(hdc, ch 2, hdc) in next ch-1 sp] around; join with sl st to first hdc (2nd ch of beg ch-4). (24 hdc & 12 ch-2 sps)

ROUND 3: Ch 1 (NOT counted as first st), sc in sp between last and first hdc (sp directly under join), 8 hdc in next ch-2 sp, *sc in sp between next 2 hdc, 8 hdc in next ch-2 sp; rep from * around; join with sl st to first sc. (12 petals & 12 sc) Fasten off Color B and weave in all ends.

Materials
Hook: E-4 (3.50 mm)

DMC Natura Just Cotton:
Color A – N 35 Nacar
Color B – N 03 Sable

Finished Size: 3¼" (8 cm)

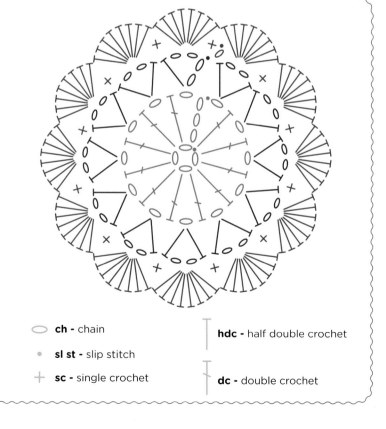

⬭ **ch -** chain	⊤ **hdc -** half double crochet
• **sl st -** slip stitch	
+ **sc -** single crochet	⊤ **dc -** double crochet

GUMIŃSKI -Dom Towarowy- STAROGARD-Chojnicka

Materials

Hook: E-4 (3.50 mm)

DMC Natura Just Cotton:
Color A – N 49 Turquoise
Color B – N 82 Lobelia
Color C – N 43 Golden Lemon
Color D – N 18 Coral
Color E – N 83 Blé

Finished Size: 5½" (14 cm)

3-Double Treble Bobble (3dtr-bob):
Wrap yarn three times around hook, insert hook into st or sp indicated, pull up lp (5 lps on hook), [yo, draw through 2 lps on hook] 3 times (2 lps on hook), *wrap yarn three times around hook, insert hook in same st or sp, pull up lp, [yo, draw through 2 lps on hook] 3 times, rep from * once more (4 lps on hook), yo and draw through all 4 lps.

3-Treble Bobble (3tr-bob): Wrap yarn twice around hook, insert hook into st or sp indicated, pull up lp (4 lps on hook), [yo, draw through 2 lps on hook] 2 times (2 lps on hook), *wrap yarn twice around hook, insert hook in same st or sp, pull up lp, [yo, draw through 2 lps on hook] 2 times, rep from * once more (4 lps on hook), yo and draw through all 4 lps.

Note: The first Bobble Stitch in a round is started differently to subsequent bobbles in round. Instructions for the first bobble are included within the pattern. For subsequent bobbles follow the instructions above.

Join with Single Crochet: With slip knot on hook, insert hook in st or sp indicated, pull up lp (2 lps on hook), yo, draw through both loops on hook (first single crochet made).

⬭	**ch -** chain
●	**sl st -** slip stitch
+	**sc -** single crochet
⊺	**dc -** double crochet
	3-bobble st
	first 4-bobble st
	3-treble bobble st

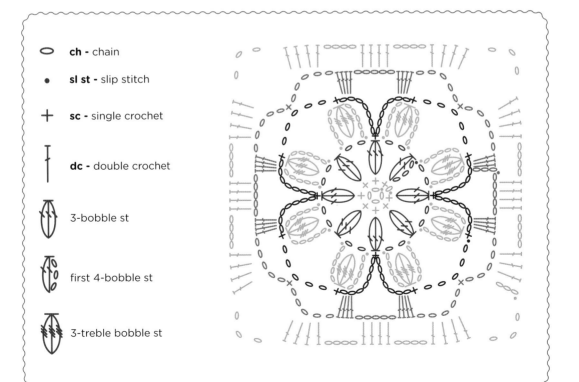

PATTERN

Base Round: Using Color A, ch 4; join with sl st to first ch to form a ring.

ROUND 1: (Right Side) Ch 1 (NOT counted as first st), 8 sc in ring; join with sl st to first sc. (8 sc) Fasten off Color A and weave in all ends.

ROUND 2: With right side facing, join Color B with sl st to any sc, ch 3 (counts as first dc, now and throughout), [yo, insert hook in same st as joining, pull up lp, yo, draw through 2 lps on hook] 2 times (3 lps on hook), yo and draw through all 3 lps (first 3-bob made), ch 2, [3-bob in next sc, ch 2] around; join with sl st to first dc (3rd ch of beg ch-3). (8 bobbles & 8 ch-2 sps) Fasten off Color B and weave in all ends.

ROUND 3: With right side facing, join Color C with sl st to any ch-2 sp, ch 5, 3dtr-bob in same sp, ch 5, sl st in same sp, [(sl st, ch 5, 3dtr-bob, ch 5, sl st) in next ch-2 sp] around, join with sl st at base of beg ch-5. (8 petals) Fasten off Color C and weave in all ends.

ROUND 4: With right side facing, using Color D, join with sc to top of any petal (bobble), ch 7, sc at base between petals (in bobble on Round 2), ch 7, sc in top of next petal, ch 5, *sc in top of next petal, ch 7, sc at base between petals, ch 7, sc in top of next petal, ch 5; rep from * around; join with sl st to first sc. (8 sc, 8 ch-7 lps & 4 ch-5 lps) Fasten off Color D and weave in all ends.

ROUND 5: With right side facing, join Color E with sl st to 2nd ch-7 lp, ch 3, 3 dc in same lp, ch 5, sc in next ch-5 lp, ch 5, 4 dc in next ch-7 lp, ch 5, *4 dc in next ch-7 lp, ch 5, sc in next ch-5 lp, ch 5, 4 dc in next ch-7 lp, ch 5; rep from * around; join with sl st to first dc (3rd ch of beg ch-3). (8 groups of 4-dc & 12 ch-5 lps) Fasten off Color E and weave in all ends.

ROUND 6: With right side facing, join Color A with sl st to 2nd ch-5 lp of any corner, ch 3, 3 dc in same lp, [ch 4, 4 dc in next ch-5 lp] 2 times, ch 3, *[4 dc in next ch-5 lp, ch 4] 2 times, 4 dc in next ch-5 lp, ch 3; rep from * around; join with sl st to first dc (3rd ch of beg ch-3). (12 groups of 4-dc, 8 ch-4 lps & 4 ch-3 lps) Fasten off Color A and weave in all ends.

Cowl - Page 114

Motif 9

PATTERN

Base Round: Using Color A, ch 4; join with sl st to first ch to form a ring.

ROUND 1: (Right Side) Ch 3 (counts as first dc, now and throughout), 17 dc in ring; join with sl st to first dc (3rd ch of beg ch-3). (18 dc)

ROUND 2: Ch 1 (NOT counted as first st, now and throughout), sc in same st as joining, ch 5, [skip next 2 dc, sc in next dc, ch 5] around; join with sl st to first sc. (6 sc & 6 ch-5 lps) Fasten off Color A and weave in all ends.

ROUND 3: With right side facing, join Color B with sl st to first ch-5 lp, ch 1, (sc, hdc, dc, tr, dc, hdc, sc) in same lp, [(sc, hdc, dc, tr, dc, hdc, sc) in next ch-5 lp] around; join with sl st to first sc. (6 petals) Fasten off Color B and weave in all ends.

ROUND 4: With right side facing, join Color C with sl st to last sc of any petal, ch 3, [yo, insert hook in same sc, pull up lp, yo, draw through 2 lps on hook] 2 times (3 lps on hook), yo and draw through all 3 lps (first 3-bob made), ch 3, 3-bob in next sc (first sc of next petal), ch 2, skip next 2 sts, sc in next tr, ch 2, skip next 2 sts, *3-bob in next sc, ch 3, 3-bob in next sc, ch 2, skip next 2 sts, sc in next tr, ch 2, skip next 2 sts; rep from * around; join with sl st to first dc (3rd ch of beg ch-3). (12 bobbles, 6 sc, 12 ch-2 sps & 6 ch-3 sps) Fasten off Color C and weave in all ends.

Materials
Hook: E-4 (3.50 mm)

DMC Natura Just Cotton:
Color A – N 79 Tilleul
Color B – N 25 Aguamarina
Color C – N 30 Glicine
Color D – N 20 Jade

Finished size: 4¼" (11 cm)

3-Bobble Stitch (3-bob): Yo, insert hook into st or sp indicated, pull up lp, yo, draw through 2 lps on hook, [yo, insert hook in same st or sp, pull up lp, yo, draw through 2 lps on hook] 2 times more (4 lps on hook), yo and draw through all 4 lps.

Note: The first Bobble Stitch in a round is started differently to subsequent bobbles in round. Instructions for the first bobble are included within the pattern. For subsequent bobbles follow the instructions above.

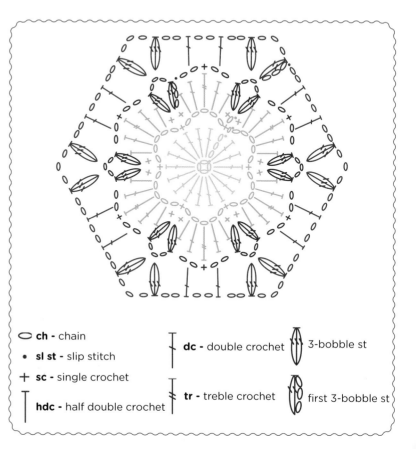

◯ **ch -** chain

• **sl st -** slip stitch

+ **sc -** single crochet

hdc - half double crochet

dc - double crochet

tr - treble crochet

3-bobble st

first 3-bobble st

ROUND 5: With right side facing, join Color D with sl st to any ch-3 sp (between bobbles), ch 3, [yo, insert hook in same sc, pull up lp, yo, draw through 2 lps on hook] 2 times (3 lps on hook), yo and draw through all 3 lps (first 3-bob made), ch 3, 3-bob in same sp, [ch 2, dc in next ch-2 sp] 2 times, ch 2, *(3-bob, ch 3, 3-bob) in next ch-3 sp, [ch 2, dc in next ch-2 sp] 2 times, ch 2; rep from * around; join with sl st to first dc (3rd ch of beg ch-3). (12 bobbles, 12 dc, 18 ch-2 sps & 6 ch-3 sps) Fasten off Color D and weave in all ends.

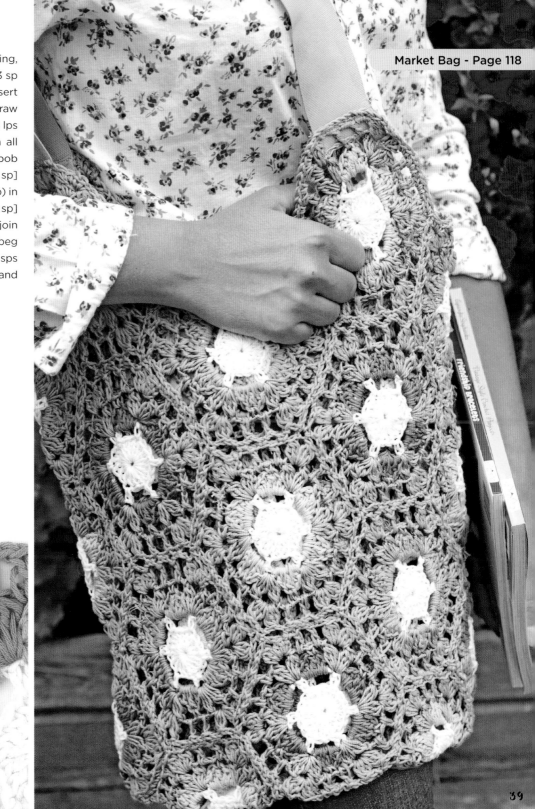

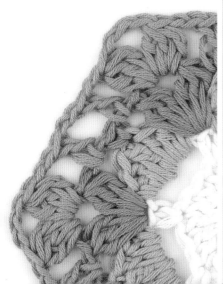

39

Motif 10

Materials

Hook: E-4 (3.50 mm)

DMC Natura Just Cotton:
Color A – N 80 Salomé
Color B – N 87 Glacier

Finished Size: : 4¾" (12 cm)

2-Bobble Stitch (2-bob): Yo, insert hook into st or sp indicated, pull up lp, yo, draw through 2 lps on hook, yo, insert hook in same st or sp, pull up lp, yo, draw through 2 lps on hook (3 lps on hook), yo and draw through all 3 lps.

3-Bobble Stitch (3-bob): Yo, insert hook into st or sp indicated, pull up lp, yo, draw through 2 lps on hook, [yo, insert hook in same st or sp, pull up lp, yo, draw through 2 lps on hook] 2 times more (4 lps on hook), yo and draw through all 4 lps.

Note: The first Bobble Stitch in a round is started differently to subsequent bobbles in round. Instructions for the first bobble are included within the pattern. For subsequent bobbles follow the instructions above.

Join with Single Crochet: With slip knot on hook, insert hook in st or sp indicated, pull up lp (2 lps on hook), yo, draw through both loops on hook (first single crochet made).

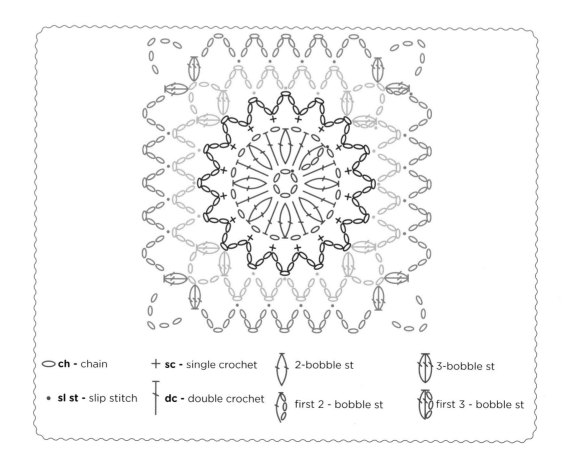

◯ **ch -** chain	✚ **sc -** single crochet	◇ 2-bobble st	◇ 3-bobble st
• **sl st -** slip stitch	**dc -** double crochet	first 2 - bobble st	first 3 - bobble st

40

PATTERN

Base Round: Using either Color A or Color B, ch 6; join with sl st to first ch to form a ring.

ROUND 1: (Right Side) Ch 3 (counts as first dc, now and throughout), yo, insert hook in ring, pull up lp, yo, draw through 2 lps on hook (2 lps on hook), yo and draw through all lps (first 2-bob made), ch 1, dc in ring, ch 1, [2-bob in ring, ch 1, dc in ring, ch 1] 7 times; join with sl st to first dc (3rd ch of beg ch-3). (8 bobbles, 8 dc & 16 ch-1 sps) Fasten off and weave in all ends.

ROUND 2: With right side facing, using next Color, join with sc to any ch-1 sp, ch 5, [sc in next ch-1 sp, ch 5] around; join with sl st to first sc. (16 sc & 16 ch-5 lps)

ROUND 3: Sl st in next ch-5 lp, ch 3 (counts as first dc, now and throughout), [yo, insert hook in same lp, pull up lp, yo, draw through 2 lps on hook] 2 times (3 lps on hook), yo and draw through all 3 lps (first 3-bob made), ch 5, 3-bob in same lp, ch 5, [in next lp, skip next 2 ch, sl st in next (center) ch, ch 5] 3 times, *(3-bob, ch 5, 3-bob) in next lp, ch 5, [sl st in center ch of next lp, ch 5] 3 times; rep from * around; join with sl st to first dc (3rd ch of beg ch-3). (8 bobbles & 20 ch-5 lps)

ROUND 4: Sl st in next ch-5 lp, ch 3, [yo, insert hook in same lp, pull up lp, yo, draw through 2 lps on hook] 2 times (3 lps on hook), yo and draw through all 3 lps (first 3-bob made), ch 5, 3-bob in same lp, ch 5, [sl st in center ch of next lp, ch 5] 4 times, *(3-bob, ch 5, 3-bob) in next lp, ch 5, [sl st in center ch of next lp, ch 5] 4 times; rep from * around; join with sl st to first dc (3rd ch of beg ch-3). (8 bobbles & 24 ch-5 lps) Fasten off and weave in all ends.

Scarf - Page 120

Motif 11

Materials
Hook: E-4 (3.50 mm)

DMC Natura Just Cotton:
Color A – N 06 Rose Layette
Color B – N 44 Agatha

Finished Size: 4¾" (12 cm)

3-Bobble Stitch (3-bob): Yo, insert hook into st or sp indicated, pull up lp, yo, draw through 2 lps on hook, [yo, insert hook in same st or sp, pull up lp, yo, draw through 2 lps on hook] 2 times more (4 lps on hook), yo and draw through all 4 lps.

3-Treble Bobble (3tr-bob): Wrap yarn twice around hook, insert hook into st or sp indicated, pull up lp (4 lps on hook), [yo, draw through 2 lps on hook] 2 times (2 lps on hook), *wrap yarn twice around hook, insert hook in same st or sp, pull up lp, [yo, draw through 2 lps on hook] 2 times, rep from * once more (4 lps on hook), yo and draw through all 4 lps.

Note: The first Bobble Stitch in a round is started differently to subsequent bobbles in round. Instructions for the first bobble are included within the pattern. For subsequent bobbles follow the instructions above.

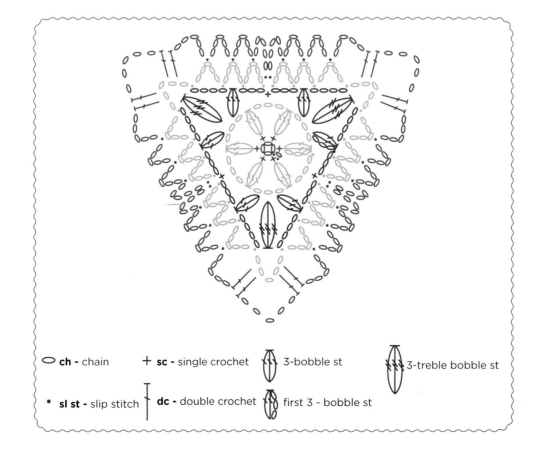

⬭ **ch** - chain   ✛ **sc** - single crochet   🮰 3-bobble st   🮰 3-treble bobble st

• **sl st** - slip stitch   ┃ **dc** - double crochet   🮰 first 3 - bobble st

PATTERN

Base Round: Using Color A, ch 4; join with sl st to first ch to form a ring.

ROUND 1: (Right Side) Ch 1 (NOT counted as first st), 6 sc in ring; join with sl st to first sc. (6 sc)

ROUND 2: Ch 3 (counts as first dc, now and throughout), [yo, insert hook in same st as joining, pull up lp, yo, draw through 2 lps on hook] 2 times (3 lps on hook), yo and draw through all 3 lps (first 3-bob made), ch 3, [3-bob in next sc, ch 3] around; join with sl st to first dc (3rd ch of beg ch-3). (6 bobbles & 6 ch-3 sps)

ROUND 3: Sl st in next ch-3 sp, ch 3, [yo, insert hook in same st as joining, pull up lp, yo, draw through 2 lps on hook] 2 times (3 lps on hook), yo and draw through all 3 lps (first 3-bob made), ch 4, (3tr-bob, ch 4, 3-bob) in same sp, ch 3, sc in next ch-3 sp, ch 3, *(3-bob, ch 4, 3tr-bob, ch 4, 3-bob) in next ch-3 sp, ch 3, sc in next ch-3 sp, ch 3; rep from * around; join with sl st to first dc (3rd ch of beg ch-3). (9 bobbles, 3 sc, 6 ch-4 sps & 6 ch-3 sps) Fasten off Color A and weave in all ends.

ROUND 4: With right side facing, join Color B with sl st to last ch-3 sp made (before first 3-bob of bobble group), ch 5, sl st in same sp, ch 5, [(sl st, ch 5, sl st) in next ch-sp, ch 5] 3 times, (sl st, ch 5, sl st) in next ch-3 sp, *[(sl st, ch 5, sl st) in next ch-sp, ch 5] 5 times, (sl st, ch 5, sl st) in next ch-3 sp; rep from * around; join with sl st in first ch. (18 ch-5 lps)

ROUND 5: *[Ch 5, sl st in next ch-5 lp] 3 times, ch 5, (2 dc, ch 5, 2 dc) in next ch-5 lp, [ch 5, sl st in next ch-5 lp] 3 times, ch 5, sl st in sp between next 2 sl sts; rep from * around. Fasten off Color B and weave in all ends.

Doily - Page 124

Motif 12

PATTERN

Base Round: Using Color A, ch 4; join with sl st to first ch to form a ring.

ROUND 1: (Right Side) Ch 1 (NOT counted as first st), 8 sc in ring; join with sl st to first sc. (8 sc) Fasten off Color A and weave in all ends.

ROUND 2: With right side facing, join Color B with sl st to any sc, ch 4, 3tr-bob in same sc, ch 4, sl st in same sc, [(sl st, ch 4, 3tr-bob, ch 4, sl st) in next sc] around; join with sl st to first ch. (8 petals) Fasten off Color B and weave in all ends.

ROUND 3: With right side facing, join Color C with sl st to any sl st (between petals), ch 3 (counts as first dc, now and throughout), dc in same st, ch 3, *2 dc in next sl st (between petals), ch 3; rep from * around; join with sl st to first dc (3rd ch of beg ch-3). (16 dc & 8 ch-3 sps) Fasten off Color C and weave in all ends.

ROUND 4: With right side facing, join Color D with sl st to any ch-3 sp, ch 3, (2 dc, ch 1, 3 dc) in same sp, ch 2, sc in next ch-3 sp, ch 2, *(3 dc, ch 1, 3 dc) in next ch-3 sp, ch 2, sc in next ch-3 sp, ch 2; rep from * around; join with sl st to first dc (3rd ch of beg ch-3). (24 dc, 4 ch-1 sps, 4 sc & 8 ch-2 sps) Fasten off Color D and weave in all ends.

Materials
Hook: E-4 (3.50 mm)

DMC Natura Just Cotton:
Color A – N 43 Golden Lemon
Color B – N 82 Lobelia
Color C – N 25 Aguamarina
Color D – N 76 Bamboo

Finished Size: 2¾" (7 cm)

3-Treble Bobble (3tr-bob): Wrap yarn twice around hook, insert hook into st or sp indicated, pull up lp (4 lps on hook), [yo, draw through 2 lps on hook] 2 times (2 lps on hook), *wrap yarn twice around hook, insert hook in same st or sp, pull up lp, [yo, draw through 2 lps on hook] 2 times, rep from * once more (4 lps on hook), yo and draw through all 4 lps.

Note: The first Bobble Stitch in a round is started differently to subsequent bobbles in round. Instructions for the first bobble are included within the pattern. For subsequent bobbles follow the directions above.

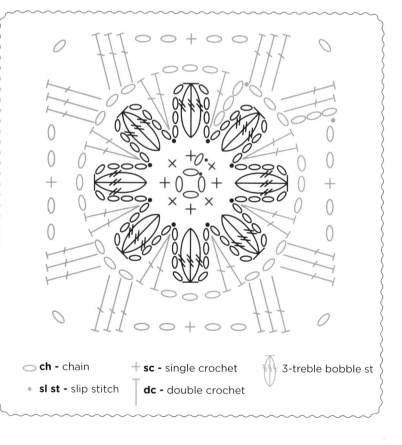

⬯ **ch** - chain   ✛ **sc** - single crochet   ⬮ **3-treble bobble st**

• **sl st** - slip stitch | **dc** - double crochet

Motif 13

PATTERN

Base Round: Using Color A, ch 4; join with sl st to first ch to form a ring.

ROUND 1: (Right Side) Ch 1 (NOT counted as first st, now and throughout), 8 sc in ring; join with sl st to first sc. (8 sc)

ROUND 2: Ch 1, sc in same st as joining, ch 5, [sc in next sc, ch 5] around; join with sl st to first sc. (8 sc & 8 ch-5 lps) Fasten off Color A and weave in all ends.

ROUND 3: With right side facing, join Color B with sl st to any ch-5 lp, ch 3 (counts as first dc), (dc, ch 1, 2 dc) in same lp, 2 hdc in next ch-5 lp, *(2 dc, ch 1, 2 dc) in next ch-5 lp, 2 hdc in next ch-5 lp; rep from * around; join with sl st to first dc (3rd ch of beg ch-3). Fasten off Color B and weave in all ends.

Materials
Hook: H-8 (5.00 mm)

DMC Natura XL:
Color A - 07 – Blue Green
Color B - 111 – Light Brown

Finished Size: 3½" (9 cm)

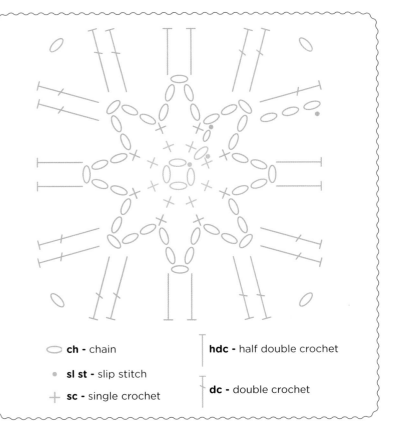

⬯ **ch -** chain

• **sl st -** slip stitch

✕ **sc -** single crochet

┬ **hdc -** half double crochet

╪ **dc -** double crochet

Sunshine Pillow - Page 128

Motif 14

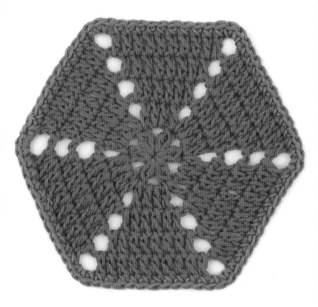

Materials
Hook: E-4 (3.50 mm)

DMC Natura Just Cotton:
Color A – N 18 Coral
Color B – N 26 Blue Jeans

Finished Size: 4¾" (12 cm)

2-Bobble Stitch (2-bob): Yo, insert hook into st or sp indicated, pull up lp, yo, draw through 2 lps on hook, yo, insert hook in same st or sp, pull up lp, yo, draw through 2 lps on hook (3 lps on hook), yo and draw through all 3 lps.

Note: The first Bobble Stitch in a round is started differently to subsequent bobbles in round. Instructions for the first bobble are included within the pattern. For subsequent bobbles follow the instructions above.

PATTERN

Base Round: Using Color A, ch 4; join with sl st to first ch to form a ring.
ROUND 1: (Right Side) Ch 3 (counts as first dc, now and throughout), yo, insert hook in ring, pull up lp, yo, draw through 2 lps on hook (2 lps on hook), yo and draw through all lps (first 2-bob made), ch 3, [2-bob in ring, ch 3] 5 times; join with sl st to first dc (3rd ch of beg ch-3). (6 bobbles & 6 ch-3 sps)
ROUND 2: Ch 6, (counts as first dc & ch-3, now and throughout), dc in same st as joining, 2 dc in next ch-3 sp, *(dc, ch 3, dc) in next bobble, 2 dc in next ch-3 sp; rep from * around; join with sl st to first dc (3rd ch of beg ch-6). (24 dc & 6 ch-3 sps)
ROUND 3: Sl st in ch-3 sp, ch 6, dc in same sp, dc in each of next 4 dc, *(dc, ch 3, dc) in next ch-3 sp, dc in each of next 4 dc; rep from * around; join with sl st to first dc (3rd ch of beg ch-6). (36 dc & 6 ch-3 sps)
ROUND 4: Sl st in ch-3 sp, ch 6, dc in same sp, dc in each of next 6 dc, *(dc, ch 3, dc) in next ch-3 sp, dc in each of next 6 dc; rep from * around; join with sl st to first dc (3rd ch of beg ch-6). (48 dc & 6 ch-3 sps)
ROUND 5: Sl st in ch-3 sp, ch 6, dc in same sp, dc in each of next 8 dc, *(dc, ch 3, dc) in next ch-3 sp, dc in each of next 8 dc; rep from * around; join with sl st to first dc (3rd ch of beg ch-6). (60 dc & 6 ch-3 sps) Fasten off Color A and weave in all ends.
ROUND 6: With right side facing, join Color B with sl st to any ch-3 sp, ch 1 (NOT counted as first st), 3 sc in same sp, sc in each of next 10 sc, *3 sc in next corner ch-3 sp, sc in each of next 10 sc; rep from * around; join with sl st to first sc. (78 sc) Fasten off Color B and weave in all ends.

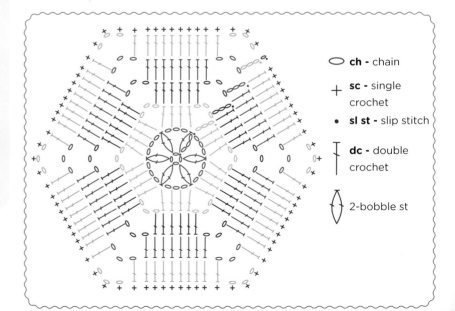

⬮	**ch -** chain
+	**sc -** single crochet
•	**sl st -** slip stitch
†	**dc -** double crochet
⬙	2-bobble st

PATTERN

Base Round: Using Color A, ch 4; join with sl st to first ch to form a ring.

ROUND 1: (Right Side) Ch 3 (counts as first dc, now and throughout), [yo, insert hook in ring, pull up lp, yo, draw through 2 lps on hook] 2 times (3 lps on hook), yo and draw through all 3 lps (first 3-bob made), ch 3, [3-bob in ring, ch 3] 5 times; join with sl st to first dc (3rd ch of beg ch-3). (6 bobbles & 6 ch-3 sps) Fasten off Color A and weave in all ends.

ROUND 2: With right side facing, join Color B with sl st to any ch-3 sp, ch 3, [yo, insert hook in same sp, pull up lp, yo, draw through 2 lps on hook] 2 times (3 lps on hook), yo and draw through all 3 lps (first 3-bob made), ch 2, 3-bob in next sp, ch 2, 3-bob in same sp, ch 2, *(3-bob, ch 2, 3-bob) in next ch-3 sp, ch 2; rep from * around; join with sl st to first dc (3rd ch of beg ch-3). (12 bobbles & 12 ch-2 sps)

ROUND 3: Sl st in next ch-2 sp, ch 3, [yo, insert hook in same sp, pull up lp, yo, draw through 2 lps on hook] 2 times (3 lps on hook), yo and draw through all 3 lps (first 3-Bobble made), ch 2, 3-bob in same sp, ch 2, 3-bob in next ch-2 sp, ch 2, *(3-bob, ch 2, 3-bob) in next ch-2 sp, ch 2, 3-bob in next ch-2 sp, ch 2; rep from * around; join with sl st to first dc (3rd ch of beg ch-3). (18 bobbles & 18 ch-2 sps)

ROUND 4: Sl st in next ch-2 sp, ch 3, [yo, insert hook in same sp, pull up lp, yo, draw through 2 lps on hook] 2 times (3 lps on hook), yo and draw through all 3 lps (first 3-bob made), ch 2, 3-bob in same sp, ch 1, [3 dc in next ch-2 sp, ch 1] 2 times, *(3-bob, ch 2, 3-bob) in next ch-2 sp, ch 1, [3 dc in next ch-2 sp, ch 1] 2 times; rep from * around; join with sl st to first dc (3rd ch of beg ch-3). (12 bobbles, 36 dc, 18 ch-1 sps & 6 ch-2 sps) Fasten off Color B and weave in all ends.

ROUND 5: With right side facing, join Color C with sl st to any corner ch-2 sp, ch 1 (NOT counted as first st), 3 sc in same sp, [sc in next st or sp] around, working 3 sc in each corner ch-2 sp; join with sl st to first sc. (84 sc) Fasten off Color C and weave in all ends.

Materials
Hook: E-4 (3.50 mm)

DMC Natura Just Cotton Colors:
Color A – N 75 Moss Green
Color B – N 03 Sable
Color C – N 26 Blue Jeans

Finished Size: 4¾" (12 cm)

3-Bobble Stitch (3-bob): Yo, insert hook into st or sp indicated, pull up lp, yo, draw through 2 lps on hook, [yo, insert hook in same st or sp, pull up lp, yo, draw through 2 lps on hook] 2 times more (4 lps on hook), yo and draw through all 4 lps.

Note: The first Bobble Stitch in a round is started differently to subsequent bobbles in round. Instructions for the first bobble are included within the pattern. For subsequent bobbles follow the directions above.

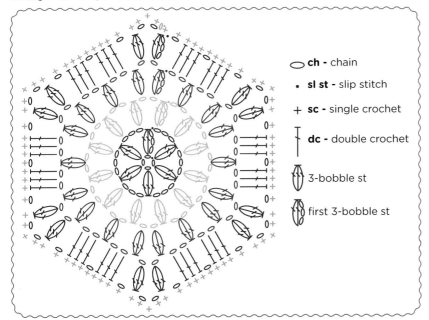

- ⬭ **ch** - chain
- • **sl st** - slip stitch
- + **sc** - single crochet
- **dc** - double crochet
- **3-bobble st**
- **first 3-bobble st**

Motif 16

Materials
Hook: E-4 (3.50 mm)

DMC Natura Just Cotton:
Color A – N 43 Golden Lemon
Color B – N 22 Tropic Brown

Finished size: 4¾" (12cm)

3-Bobble Stitch (3-bob): Yo, insert hook into st or sp indicated, pull up lp, yo, draw through 2 lps on hook, [yo, insert hook in same st or sp, pull up lp, yo, draw through 2 lps on hook] 2 times more (4 lps on hook), yo and draw through all 4 lps.

Note: The first Bobble Stitch in a round is started differently to subsequent bobbles in round. Instructions for the first bobble are included within the pattern. For subsequent bobbles follow the instructions above.

Join with Single Crochet: With slip knot on hook, insert hook in st or sp indicated, pull up lp (2 lps on hook), yo, draw through both loops on hook (first single crochet made).

PATTERN

Base Round: Using Color A, ch 4; join with sl st to first ch to form a ring.

ROUND 1: (Right Side) Ch 3 (counts as first dc, now and throughout), [yo, insert hook in ring, pull up lp, yo, draw through 2 lps on hook] 2 times (3 lps on hook), yo and draw through all 3 lps (first 3-bob made), ch 3, [3-bob in ring, ch 3] 5 times; join with sl st to first dc (3rd ch of beg ch-3). (6 bobbles & 6 ch-3 sps)

ROUND 2: Ch 3, [yo, insert hook in same st as joining, pull up lp, yo, draw through 2 lps on hook] 2 times (3 lps on hook), yo and draw through all 3 lps (first 3-bob made), ch 2, 3-bob in next ch-3 sp, ch 2, *3-bob in next bobble, ch 2, 3-bob in next ch-3 sp, ch 2; rep from * around; join with sl st to first dc (3rd ch of beg ch-3). (12 bobbles & 12 ch-2 sps)

ROUND 3: Ch 3, [yo, insert hook in same st as joining, pull up lp, yo, draw through 2 lps on hook] 2 times (3 lps on hook), yo and draw through all 3 lps (first 3-bob made), ch 2, [dc in next ch-2 sp, ch 2] 2 times, *3-bob in next bobble, ch 2, [dc in next ch-2 sp, ch 2] 2 times; rep from * around; join with sl st to first dc (3rd ch of beg ch-3). (6 bobbles, 12 dc & 18 ch-2 sps)

ROUND 4: Ch 3, [yo, insert hook in same st as joining, pull up lp, yo, draw through 2 lps on hook] 2 times (3 lps on hook), yo and draw through all 3 lps (first 3-bob made), ch 2, dc in next ch-2 sp, ch 2, 3-bob in next ch-2 sp, ch 2, dc in next ch-2 sp, ch2, *3-bob in next bobble, ch 2, dc in next ch-2 sp, ch 2, 3-bob in next ch-2 sp, ch 2, dc in next ch-2 sp, ch2; rep from * around; join with sl st to first dc (3rd ch of beg ch-3). (12 bobbles, 12 dc & 24 ch-2 sps) Fasten off Color A and weave in all ends.

ROUND 5: With right side facing, using Color B, join with sc to any ch-2 sp, 2 sc in same sp, [3 sc in next ch-2 sp] around; join with sl st to first sc. (72 sc)

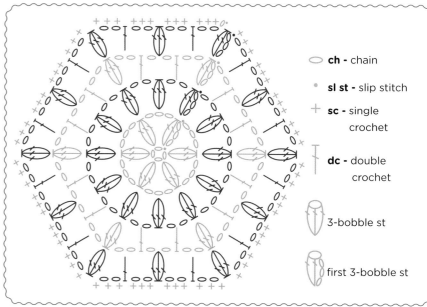

◯ **ch -** chain

• **sl st -** slip stitch

+ **sc -** single crochet

| **dc -** double crochet

3-bobble st

first 3-bobble st

50

PATTERN

Base Round: Using Color A, ch 4; join with sl st to first ch to form a ring.
ROUND 1: (Right Side) Ch 3 (counts as first dc, now and throughout), yo, insert hook in ring, pull up lp, yo, draw through 2 lps on hook (2 lps on hook), yo and draw through both lps (first 2-bob made), ch 3, 2-bob in ring, ch 1 *2-bob in ring, ch 3, 2-bob in ring, ch 3; rep from * 2 times more; join with sl st to first dc (3rd ch of beg ch-3). (8 bobbles, 4 ch-3 sps & 4 ch-1 sps)

ROUND 2: Sl st in first ch-3 sp, ch 3, [yo, insert hook in same sp, pull up lp, yo, draw through 2 lps on hook] 2 times (3 lps on hook), yo and draw through all 3 lps (first 3-bob made), ch 3, 3-bob in same sp, ch 1, 2 dc in next ch-1 sp, ch 1, * (3-bob, ch 3, 3-bob) in next ch-3 sp, ch 1, 2 dc in next ch-1 sp,ch 1; rep from * around; join with sl st to first dc (3rd ch of beg ch-3). (8 bobbles, 8 dc, 8 ch-1 sps & 4 ch-3 sps)

ROUND 3: Sl st in first ch-3 sp, ch 3, [yo, insert hook in same sp, pull up lp, yo, draw through 2 lps on hook] 2 times (3 lps on hook), yo and draw through all 3 lps (first 3-bob made), ch 3, 3-bob in same sp, ch 1, [2 dc in next ch-1 sp, ch 1] 2 times, * (3-bob, ch 3, 3-bob) in next ch-3 sp, ch 1, [2 dc in next ch-1 sp,ch 1] 2 times; rep from * around; join with sl st to first dc (3rd ch of beg ch-3). (8 bobbles, 16 dc, 12 ch-1 sps & 4 ch-3 sps)

ROUND 4: Sl st in first ch-3 sp, ch 3, [yo, insert hook in same sp, pull up lp, yo, draw through 2 lps on hook] 2 times (3 lps on hook), yo and draw through all 3 lps (first 3-bob made), ch 3, 3-bob in same sp, ch 1, [2 dc in next ch-1 sp, ch 1] 3 times, * (3-bob, ch 3, 3-bob) in next ch-3 sp, ch 1, [2 dc in next ch-1 sp,ch 1] 3 times; rep from * around; join with sl st to first dc (3rd ch of beg ch-3). (8 bobbles, 24 dc, 16 ch-1 sps & 4 ch-3 sps) Fasten off and weave in all ends.

Materials
Hook: E-4 (3.50 mm)

DMC Natura Just Cotton:
Color A – N 16 Tournesol

Finished size: 4″ (10 cm)

2-Bobble Stitch (2-bob): Yo, insert hook into st or sp indicated, pull up lp, yo, draw through 2 lps on hook, yo, insert hook in same st or sp, pull up lp, yo, draw through 2 lps on hook (3 lps on hook), yo and draw through all 3 lps.

3-Bobble Stitch (3-bob): Yo, insert hook into st or sp indicated, pull up lp, yo, draw through 2 lps on hook, [yo, insert hook in same st or sp, pull up lp, yo, draw through 2 lps on hook] 2 times more (4 lps on hook), yo and draw through all 4 lps.

Note: The first Bobble Stitch in a round is started differently to subsequent bobbles in round. Instructions for the first bobble are included within the pattern. For subsequent bobbles follow the instructions above.

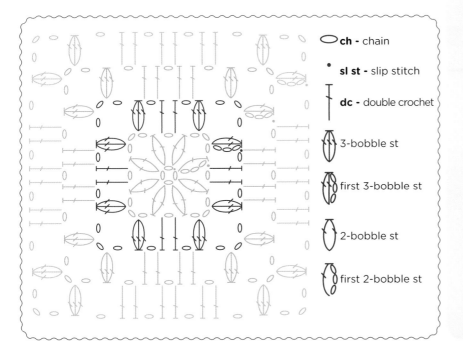

⬭ **ch** - chain

• **sl st** - slip stitch

┬ **dc** - double crochet

⬭ 3-bobble st

first 3-bobble st

2-bobble st

first 2-bobble st

Motif 18

PATTERN

Base Round: Using Color A, ch 4; join with sl st to first ch to form a ring.

ROUND 1: (Right Side) Ch 3 (counts as first dc, now and throughout), 2 dc in ring, drop lp from hook, insert hook from front to back in first dc (3rd ch of beg ch-3), pull dropped lp through (first popcorn made), ch 1, dc in ring, ch 1, PC in ring, ch 3, * PC in ring, ch 1, dc in ring, ch 1, PC in ring, ch 3; rep from * around; join with sl st to first dc (3rd ch of beg ch-3). (8 popcorns, 4 dc, 8 ch-1 sps & 4 ch-3 sps)

ROUND 2: Sl st in next ch-1 sp, ch 6 (counts as first dc & ch-3), sc in next dc, ch 3, dc in next ch-1 sp, ch 2, (PC, ch 3, PC) in next ch-3 sp, ch 2, *dc in next ch-1 sp, ch 3, sc in next dc, ch 3, dc in next ch-1 sp, ch 2, (PC, ch 3, PC) in next ch-3 sp, ch 2; rep from * around; join with sl st to first dc (3rd ch of beg ch-3). (8 popcorns, 8 dc, 4 sc, 8 ch-2 sps & 12 ch-3 sps)

ROUND 3: Sl st in next ch-3 sp (before sc), ch 5 (counts as first dc & ch-2), dc in next ch-3 sp (after sc), ch 2, dc in next ch-2 sp, ch 2, (PC, ch 3, PC) in next ch-3 sp, ch 2, dc om next ch-2 sp, ch 2, *[dc in next ch-3 sp, ch 2] 2 times, dc in next ch-2 sp, ch 2, (PC, ch 3, PC) in next ch-3 sp, ch 2; rep from * around; join with sl st to first dc (3rd ch of beg ch-3). (8 popcorns, 16 dc, 20 ch-2 sps & 4 ch-3 sps) Fasten off and weave in all ends.

Materials

Hook: E-4 (3.50 mm)

DMC Natura Just Cotton:
Color A – N 86 Brique

Finished size: 4″ (10 cm)

Popcorn (PC): 3 dc in same st or sp indicted, drop lp from hook, insert hook from front to back in first dc made, pull dropped lp through.

Note: The first Popcorn Stitch in a round is started differently to subsequent popcorns in round. Instructions for the first popcorn are included within the pattern. For subsequent popcorns follow the instructions above.

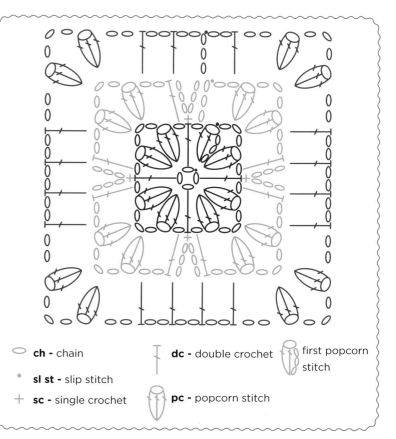

⬭	**ch -** chain	⊤	**dc -** double crochet	first popcorn stitch
•	**sl st -** slip stitch			
+	**sc -** single crochet		**pc -** popcorn stitch	

PATTERN

Base Round: Using Color A, ch 4; join with sl st to first ch to form a ring.

ROUND 1: (Right Side) Ch 1 (NOT counted as first st), 8 sc in ring; join with sl st to first sc. (8 sc)

ROUND 2: *Ch 9, sl st in each of next 2 sc; rep from * around (the last sl st will be at base of beg ch-9). (4 ch-9 lps)

ROUND 3: Sl st in ch-9 lp, ch 3 (counts as first dc, now and throughout), (15 dc, sl st) in same lp, *(sl st, ch 3, 15 dc, sl st) in next ch-9 lp; rep from * around; join with sl st to first sl st. (4 petals – with 16 dc each)

ROUND 4: Ch 6 (counts as first dc & ch-3), skip first 3 dc, sc in next (4th) dc, ch 3, skip next 3 dc, (dc, ch 3, dc) in next (8th) dc, ch 3, skip next 3 dc, sc in next (12th) dc, ch 3, *dc between petals, ch 3, skip next 3 dc, sc in next dc, ch 3, skip next 3 dc, (dc, ch 3, dc) in next dc, ch 3, skip next 3 dc, sc in next dc, ch 3; rep from * around; join with sl st to first dc (3rd ch of beg ch-3). Fasten off and weave in all ends.

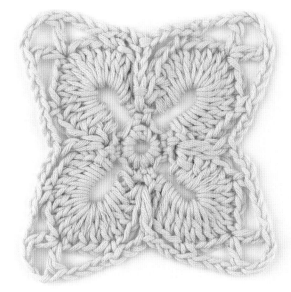

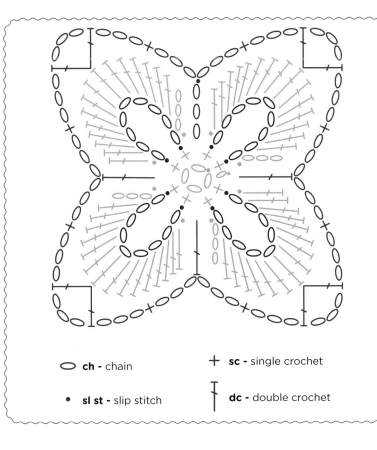

○ **ch -** chain

• **sl st -** slip stitch

+ **sc -** single crochet

┬ **dc -** double crochet

Materials
Hook: E-4 (3.50 mm)

DMC Natura Just Cotton:
Color A – N 87 Glacier

Finished size: 3½" (9 cm)

Motif 20

PATTERN

Base Round: Using Color A, ch 4; join with sl st to first ch to form a ring.

ROUND 1: (Right Side) Ch 1 (NOT counted as first st, now and throughout), 8 sc in ring; join with sl st to first sc. (8 sc) Fasten off Color A and weave in all ends.

ROUND 2: With right side facing, join Color B with sl st to any sc, [ch 5, sl st in each of next 2 sc] around (the last sl st will be at base of beg ch-5). (4 ch-5 lps)

ROUND 3: *(Sl st, ch 1, 7 dc, sl st) in next ch-5 lp, sc between lps; rep from * around; join with sl st to first sl st. (4 petals) Fasten off Color B and weave in all ends.

ROUND 4: With right side facing, join Color A with sl st to any sc, ch 6 (counts as first dc and ch-3), skip next 2 dc, sc in next (3rd) dc, ch 2, sc in next dc, ch 3, *skip next 3 dc, dc in next sc, ch 3, skip next 2 dc, sc in next dc, ch 2, sc in next dc, ch 3; rep from * around; join with sl st to first dc (3rd ch of beg ch-3). (4 dc, 8 sc, 4 ch-2 sps & 8 ch-3 sps)

ROUND 5: Ch 1, *3 sc in next ch-3 sp, (sc, ch 1, sc) in next ch-2 sp, 3 sc in next ch-3 sp; rep from * around; join with sl st to first sc. (32 sc & 4 ch-1 sps) Fasten off Color A and weave in all ends.

Materials
Hook: H-8 (5.00 mm)

DMC Natura XL:
Color A – 10 Orange
Color B – 71 Blue

Finished size: 4¾" (12 cm)

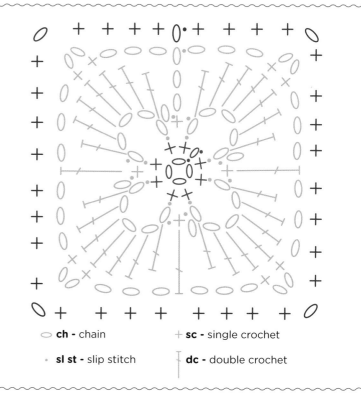

○ **ch** - chain   + **sc** - single crochet

· **sl st** - slip stitch   ╎ **dc** - double crochet

Motif 21

PATTERN

Base Round: Using Color A, ch 4; join with sl st to first ch to form a ring.

ROUND 1: (Right Side) Ch 1 (NOT counted as first st), 12 sc in ring; join with sl st to first sc. (12 sc) Fasten off Color A and weave in all ends. Join with a sl st into top of beginning ch-1. Fasten off.

ROUND 2: With right side facing, join Color B with sl st to any sc, ch 4 (counts as first tr), tr in same st as joining, [2 tr in next sc] around; join with sl st to first tr (4th ch of beg ch-4). (24 tr) Fasten off Color B and weave in all ends.

ROUND 3: With right side facing, join Color C with sl st to sp between any 2-tr group, ch 3 (counts as first dc, now and throughout), [yo, insert hook in same st as joining, pull up lp, yo, draw through 2 lps on hook] 2 times (3 lps on hook), yo and draw through all 3 lps (first 3-bob made), ch 3, *3-bob in next sp between 2-tr groups, ch 3; rep from * around; join with sl st to first dc (3rd ch of beg ch-3). (12 bobbles & 12 ch-3 sps) Fasten off Color C and weave in all ends.

ROUND 4: With right side facing, join Color D with sl st in any ch-3 sp, ch 3, (dc, ch 1, 2 dc) in same sp, 3 hdc in each of next 2 ch-3 sps, *(2 dc, ch 1, 2 dc) in next ch-3 sp, 3 hdc in each of next 2 ch-3 sps; rep from * around; join with sl st to first dc (3rd ch of beg ch-3). (16 dc, 24 hdc & 4 ch-1 sps) Fasten off Color D and weave in all ends.

Materials

Hook: E-4 (3.50 mm)

DMC Natura Just Cotton:
Color A – N 75 Moss Green
Color B – N 79 Tilleul
Color C – N 06 Rose Layette
Color D – N 76 Bamboo

Finished Size: 3¼" (9 cm)

3-Bobble Stitch (3-bob): Yo, insert hook into st or sp indicated, pull up lp, yo, draw through 2 lps on hook, [yo, insert hook in same st or sp, pull up lp, yo, draw through 2 lps on hook] 2 times more (4 lps on hook), yo and draw through all 4 lps.

Note: The first Bobble Stitch in a round is started differently to subsequent bobbles in round. Instructions for the first bobble are included within the pattern. For subsequent bobbles follow the directions above.

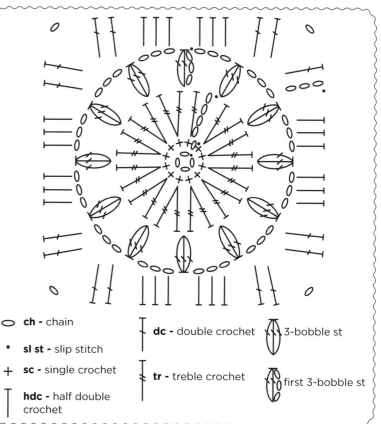

ch - chain

sl st - slip stitch

sc - single crochet

hdc - half double crochet

dc - double crochet

tr - treble crochet

3-bobble st

first 3-bobble st

PATTERN

Base Round: Using Color A, ch 4; join with sl st to first ch to form a ring.

ROUND 1: (Right Side) Ch 1 (NOT counted as first st), 8 sc in ring; join with sl st to first sc. (8 sc)

ROUND 2: Ch 9 (counts as first tr & ch-5), 3tr-bob in next sc, ch 5, *tr in next sc, ch 5, 3tr-bob in next sc, ch 5; rep from * around; join with sl st to first tr (4th ch of beg ch-9). (4 bobbles, 4 tr & 8 ch-5 lps).

ROUND 3: Ch 7 (counts as first tr & ch-4), tr in same st as joining, ch 5, sc in next ch-5 lp, ch 5, sc in next bobble, ch 5, sc in next ch-5 lp, ch 5, *(tr, ch 3, tr) in next tr, ch 5, sc in next ch-5 lp, ch 5, sc in next bobble, ch 5, sc in next ch-5 lp, ch 5; rep from * around; join with sl st to first tr (4th ch of beg ch-4). (8 tr, 12 sc, 16 ch-5 lps & 4 ch-3 sps) Fasten off and weave in all ends.

Materials
Hook: E-4 (3.50 mm)

DMC Natura Just Cotton:
Color A – N 47 Safran

Finished Size: 3½″ (9 cm)

3-Treble Bobble (3tr-bob): Wrap yarn twice around hook, insert hook into st or sp indicated, pull up lp (4 lps on hook), [yo, draw through 2 lps on hook] 2 times (2 lps on hook), *wrap yarn twice around hook, insert hook in same st or sp, pull up lp, [yo, draw through 2 lps on hook] 2 times, rep from * once more (4 lps on hook), yo and draw through all 4 lps.

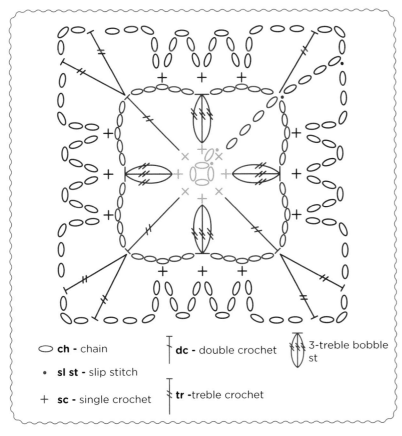

○ **ch -** chain

• **sl st -** slip stitch

+ **sc -** single crochet

dc - double crochet

tr - treble crochet

3-treble bobble st

Motif 23

PATTERN

Base Round: Using Color A, ch 6; join with sl st to first ch to form a ring.

ROUND 1: (Right Side) Ch 1 (NOT counted as first st), 18 sc in ring; join with sl st to first sc. (18 sc)

ROUND 2: Ch 4 (counts as first tr), *wrap yarn twice around hook, insert hook in next st, pull up lp, [yo, draw through 2 lps on hook] 2 times, rep from * once more (3 lps on hook), yo and draw through all 3 lps (first cluster made), ch 5, *3tr-cl (using next 3 sc), ch 5; rep from * around; join with sl st to first tr (4th ch of beg ch-4). (6 clusters & 6 ch-5 lps)

ROUND 3: Ch 3 (counts as first dc), [yo, insert hook in same st as joining, pull up lp, yo, draw through 2 lps on hook] 2 times (3 lps on hook), yo and draw through all 3 lps (first 3-bob made), ch 3, 3-bob in same st, ch 1, 3 dc in next ch-5 lp, ch 1, *(3-bob, ch 3, 3-bob) in next cluster, ch 1, 3 dc in next ch-5 lp, ch 1; rep from * around; join with sl st to first dc (3rd ch of beg ch). (12 bobbles, 18 dc, 12 ch-1 sps & 6 ch-3 sps) Fasten off and weave in all ends.

Materials
Hook: E-4 (3.50 mm)

DMC Natura Just Cotton:
Color A – N 05 Bleu Layette

Finished Size: 3½" (9 cm)

3-Bobble Stitch (3-bob): Yo, insert hook into st or sp indicated, pull up lp, yo, draw through 2 lps on hook, [yo, insert hook in same st or sp, pull up lp, yo, draw through 2 lps on hook] 2 times more (4 lps on hook), yo and draw through all 4 lps.

3-Treble Cluster (3tr-cl): Wrap yarn twice around hook, insert hook into st or sp indicated, pull up lp (4 lps on hook), [yo, draw through 2 lps on hook] 2 times (2 lps on hook), *wrap yarn twice around hook, insert hook in next st or sp, pull up lp, [yo, draw through 2 lps on hook] 2 times, rep from * once more (4 lps on hook), yo and draw through all 4 lps.

Note: The first Bobble or cluster Stitch in a round is started differently to subsequent stitches in round. Instructions for the first bobble or cluster are included within the pattern. For subsequent stitches follow the instructions above.

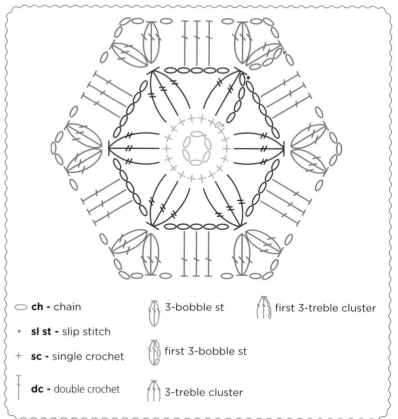

ch - chain

sl st - slip stitch

+ sc - single crochet

dc - double crochet

3-bobble st

first 3-bobble st

3-treble cluster

first 3-treble cluster

PATTERN

Base Round: Using Color A, ch 4; join with sl st to first ch to form a ring.

ROUND 1: (Right Side) Ch 1 (NOT counted as first st), 12 sc in ring; join with sl st to first sc. (12 sc)

ROUND 2: Ch 4 (counts as first tr), *wrap yarn twice around hook, insert hook in same st as joining, pull up lp, [yo, draw through 2 lps on hook] 2 times, rep from * once more (3 lps on hook), yo and draw through all 3 lps (first bobble made), ch 5, [3tr-bob in next sc, ch 5] around; join with sl st to first tr (4th ch of beg ch-4). (12 bobbles & 12 ch-5 lps) Fasten off Color A and weave in all ends.

ROUND 3: With right side facing, join Color B with sl st to any ch-5 lp, ch 6 (counts as first dc & ch-3), dc in same lp, ch 5, [sc in next lp, ch 5] 2 times, *(dc, ch 3, dc) in next ch-5 lp, ch 5, [sc in next lp, ch 5] 2 times; rep from * around; join with sl st to first dc (3rd ch of beg ch-6). (8 dc, 4 ch-3 sps, 8 sc & 12 ch-5 lps) Fasten off and weave in all ends.

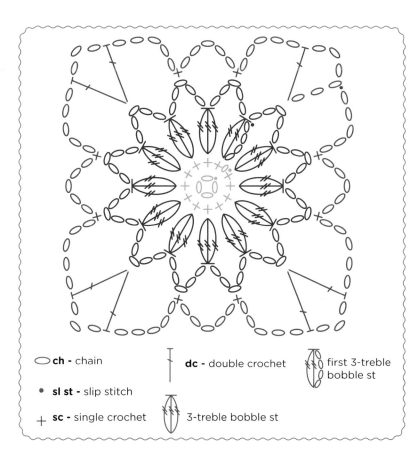

○ **ch -** chain

● **sl st -** slip stitch

+ **sc -** single crochet

| **dc -** double crochet

first 3-treble bobble st

3-treble bobble st

Materials
Hook: E-4 (3.50 mm)

DMC Natura Just Cotton:
Color A – N 16 Tournesol
Color B – N 46 Forêt

Finished Size: 3½" (9 cm)

3-Treble Bobble (3tr-bob): Wrap yarn twice around hook, insert hook into st or sp indicated, pull up lp (4 lps on hook), [yo, draw through 2 lps on hook] 2 times (2 lps on hook), *wrap yarn twice around hook, insert hook in same st or sp, pull up lp, [yo, draw through 2 lps on hook] 2 times, rep from * once more (4 lps on hook), yo and draw through all 4 lps.

Note: The first Bobble or Cluster Stitch in a round is started differently to subsequent bobbles in round. Instructions for the first bobble are included within the pattern. For subsequent bobbles follow the directions above.

PATTERN

Base Round: Using Color A, ch 4; join with sl st to first ch to form a ring.

ROUND 1: (Right Side) Ch 1 (NOT counted as first st), 8 sc in ring; join with sl st to first sc. (8 sc) Fasten off Color A and weave in all ends.

ROUND 2: With right side facing, join Color B with sl st to any sc, ch 5 (counts as first dc & ch-2), [dc in next sc, ch 2] around; join with sl st to first dc (3rd ch of beg ch-5). (8 dc & 8 ch-2 sps) Fasten off Color B and weave in all ends.

ROUND 3: With right side facing, join Color C with sl st to any ch-2 sp, ch 4 (counts as first tr), 2 tr in same sp, ch 3, 3 tr in next ch-2 sp, ch 5, *3 tr in next ch-2 sp, ch 3, 3 tr in next ch-2 sp, ch 5; rep from * around; join with sl st to first tr (4th ch of beg ch-4). (24 tr, 4 ch-3 sps & 4 ch-5 lps) Fasten off Color C and weave in all ends.

ROUND 4: With right side facing, join Color D with sl st to any ch-5 lp, ch 3 (counts as first dc), (dc, ch 3, 2 dc) in same lp, ch 3, 3 dc in next ch-3 sp, ch 3, *(2 dc, ch 3, 2 dc) in next ch-5 lp, ch 3, 3 dc in next ch-3 sp, ch 3; rep from * around; join with sl st to first dc (3rd ch of beg ch-3). (28 dc & 12 ch-3 sps) Fasten off Color D and weave in all ends.

Materials
Hook: E-4 (3.50 mm)

DMC Natura Just Cotton:
Color A – N 85 Giroflée
Color B – N 30 Glicine
Color C – N 05 Bleu Layette
Color D – N 75 Moss Green

Finished Size: 3½" (9 cm)

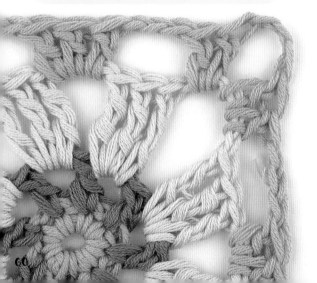

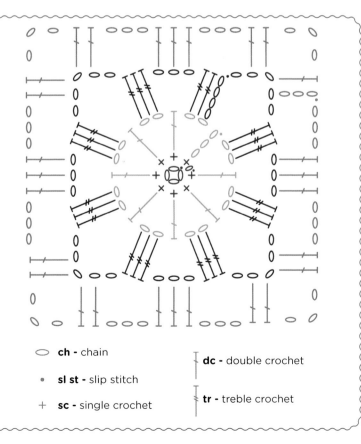

⬭ **ch -** chain

• **sl st -** slip stitch

+ **sc -** single crochet

⊤ **dc -** double crochet

‡ **tr -** treble crochet

PATTERN

Base Round: Using Color A, ch 6; join with sl st to first ch to form a ring.

ROUND 1: (Right Side) Ch 1 (NOT counted as first st, now and throughout), 18 sc in ring; join with sl st to first sc. (18 sc) Fasten off Color A and weave in all ends.

ROUND 2: With right side facing, join Color B with sl st to any sc, ch 4 (counts as first tr), *wrap yarn twice around hook, insert hook in next st, pull up lp, [yo, draw through 2 lps on hook] 2 times, rep from * once more (3 lps on hook), yo and draw through all 3 lps (first cluster made), ch 5, *3tr-cl (using next 3 sc), ch 5; rep from * around; join with sl st to first tr (4th ch of beg ch-4). (6 clusters & 6 ch-5 lps) Fasten off Color B and weave in all ends.

ROUND 3: With right side facing, join Color C with sl st to any ch-5 lp, ch 1, sc in same lp, ch 7, (dc, ch 3, dc) in next lp, ch 7, *sc in next lp, ch 7, (dc, ch 3, dc) in next lp, ch 7; rep from * around; join with sl st to first sc. (3 sc, 6 ch-7 lps, 6 dc & 3 ch-3 sps) Fasten off Color C and weave in all ends.

ROUND 4: With right side facing, join Color D with sl st to any ch-3 sp, ch 3 (counts as first dc), [yo, insert hook in ring, pull up lp, yo, draw through 2 lps on hook] 2 times (3 lps on hook), yo and draw through all 3 lps (first 3-bob made), ch 4, (3tr-bob, ch 4, 3-bob) in same sp, ch 5, sc in next ch-7 lp ch 5, (dc, ch 3, dc) in next sc, ch 5, sc in next ch-7 lp, ch 5, *(3-bob, ch 4, 3tr-bob, ch 4, 3-bob) in next ch-3 sp, ch 5, sc in next ch-7 lp ch 5, (dc, ch 3, dc) in next sc, ch 5, sc in next ch-7 lp, ch 5; rep from * around; join with sl st to first dc. (9 bobbles, 6 dc, 6 sc, 3 ch-3 sps, 6 ch-4 lps & 12 ch-5 lps) Fasten off Color D and weave in all ends.

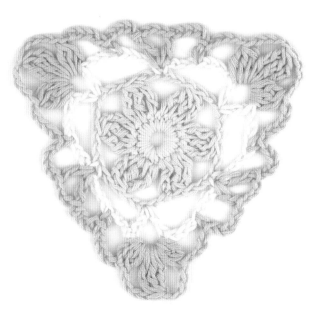

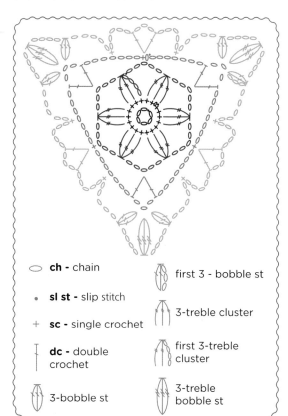

◯	**ch** - chain
•	**sl st** - slip stitch
+	**sc** - single crochet
⊤	**dc** - double crochet
	3-bobble st
	first 3 - bobble st
	3-treble cluster
	first 3-treble cluster
	3-treble bobble st

Materials

Hook: E-4 (3.50 mm)

DMC Natura just cotton:
Color A – N 06 Rose Layette
Color B – N 87 Glacier
Color C – N 79 Tilleul
Color D – N 03 Sable

Finished Size: 4¾" (12 cm)

3-Treble Cluster (3tr-cl): Wrap yarn twice around hook, insert hook into st or sp indicated, pull up lp (4 lps on hook), [yo, draw through 2 lps on hook] 2 times (2 lps on hook), *wrap yarn twice around hook, insert hook in next st or sp, pull up lp, [yo, draw through 2 lps on hook] 2 times, rep from * once more (4 lps on hook), yo and draw through all 4 lps.

3-Bobble Stitch (3-bob): Yo, insert hook into st or sp indicated, pull up lp, yo, draw through 2 lps on hook, [yo, insert hook in same st or sp, pull up lp, yo, draw through 2 lps on hook] 2 times more (4 lps on hook), yo and draw through all 4 lps.

3-Treble Bobble (3tr-bob): Wrap yarn twice around hook, insert hook into st or sp indicated, pull up lp (4 lps on hook), [yo, draw through 2 lps on hook] 2 times (2 lps on hook), *wrap yarn twice around hook, insert hook in same st or sp, pull up lp, [yo, draw through 2 lps on hook] 2 times, rep from * once more (4 lps on hook), yo and draw through all 4 lps.

Note: The first Bobble or Cluster Stitch in a round is started differently to subsequent bobbles/clusters in round. Instructions for the first bobble/cluster are included within the pattern. For subsequent bobbles/clusters follow the instructions above.

Motif 27

PATTERN

Base Round: Using Color A, ch 4; join with sl st to first ch to form a ring.

ROUND 1: (Right Side) Ch 1 (NOT counted as first st), 12 sc in ring; join with sl st to first sc. (12 sc)

ROUND 2: Ch 3 (counts as first dc, now and throughout), puff in same st as joining, [ch 2, puff in next sc] 2 times, ch 5, *puff in next sc, [ch 2, puff in next sc] 2 times, ch 5; rep from * around; join with sl st to first puff. (12 puffs, 8 ch-2 sps & 4 ch-5 lps)

ROUND 3: Sl st in first ch-2 sp, ch 3, puff in same sp, ch 2, puff in next ch-2 sp, ch 1, (2 dc, ch 3, 2 dc) in next ch-5 lp, ch 1, *puff in next ch-2 sp, ch 2, puff in next ch-2 sp, ch 1, (2 dc, ch 3, 2 dc) in next ch-5 lp, ch 1; rep from * around; join with sl st to first puff. (8 puffs, 16 dc, 4 ch-2 sps, 8 ch-1 sps & 4 ch-3 sps)

ROUND 4: Sl st in next ch-2 sp, ch 3, puff in same sp, ch 1, dc in next ch-1 sp, dc in sp between next 2 dc, (2 dc, ch 3, 2 dc) in next ch-3 sp, dc in sp between next 2 dc, dc in next ch-1 sp, ch 1, *puff in next ch-2 sp, ch 1, dc in next ch-1 sp, dc in sp between next 2 dc, (2 dc, ch 3, 2 dc) in next ch-3 sp, dc in sp between next 2 dc, dc in next ch-1 sp, ch 1,; rep from * around; join with sl st to first puff. (4 puffs, 32 dc, 8 ch-1 sps & 4 ch-3 sps) Fasten off and weave in all ends.

Materials
Hook: E-4 (3.50 mm)

DMC Natura Just Cotton:
Color A – N 09 Gris Argent

Finished Size: 3½" (9 cm)

Puff Stitch (puff): In same st or sp indicated, [yo hook, insert hook, pull up a loop (to height of dc)] 4 times, yo and draw through all 9 loops on the hook, ch 1 to secure.

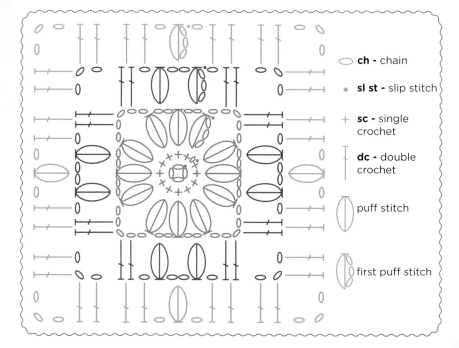

- ⬭ **ch** - chain
- • **sl st** - slip stitch
- ＋ **sc** - single crochet
- | **dc** - double crochet
- puff stitch
- first puff stitch

PATTERN

Base Round: Using Color A, ch 4; join with sl st to first ch to form a ring.

ROUND 1: (Right Side) Ch 4 (counts as first tr), wrap yarn twice around hook, insert hook in ring, pull up lp, [yo, draw through 2 lps on hook] 2 times (2 lps on hook), yo and draw through both lps (first 2tr-bob made) ch 2, [2tr-bob in ring, ch 2] 7 times; join with sl st to first tr (4th ch of beg ch-4). (8 bobbles & 8 ch-2 sps) Fasten off Color A and weave in all ends.

ROUND 2: With right side facing, join Color B with sl st to any ch-2 sp, ch 3, (2tr-bob, ch 5, 2tr-bob, ch 3, sl st) in same sp, *(sl st, ch 3, 2tr-bob, ch 5, 2tr-bob, ch 3, sl st) in next ch-2 sp; rep from * around; join with sl st to first sl st. (16 bobbles, 16 ch-3 sps & 8 ch-5 lps) Fasten off Color B and weave in all ends.

ROUND 3: With right side facing, join Color C with sl st to any bobble, ch 1 (NOT counted as first st), *(sc, hdc, 2 dc, ch 2, 2 dc, hdc, sc) in next ch-5 lp; rep from * around; join with sl st to first sc. (8 petals) Fasten off Color C and weave in all ends.

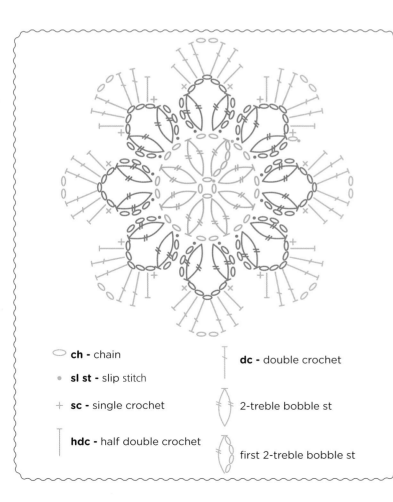

⬯ **ch -** chain

• **sl st -** slip stitch

+ **sc -** single crochet

| **hdc -** half double crochet

| **dc -** double crochet

◇ 2-treble bobble st

◇ first 2-treble bobble st

Materials
Hook: E-4 (3.50 mm)

DMC Natura Just Cotton:
Color A – N 79 Tilleul
Color B – N 76 Bamboo
Color C – N 49 Turquoise

Finished size: 4¾″ (12 cm)

2-Treble Bobble (2tr-bob): Wrap yarn twice around hook, insert hook into st or sp indicated, pull up lp (4 lps on hook), [yo, draw through 2 lps on hook] 2 times (2 lps on hook), wrap yarn twice around hook, insert hook in same st or sp, pull up lp, [yo, draw through 2 lps on hook] 2 times (3 lps on hook), yo and draw through all 3 lps.

Note: The first Bobble Stitch in a round is started differently to subsequent bobbles in round. Instructions for the first bobble are included within the pattern. For subsequent bobbles follow the instructions above.

Motif 29

PATTERN

Base Round: Using Color A, ch 6; join with sl st to first ch to form a ring.

ROUND 1: (Right Side) Ch 3 (counts as first dc, now and throughout), 23 dc in ring; join with sl st to first dc (3rd ch of beg ch-3). (24 dc) Fasten off Color A and weave in all ends.

ROUND 2: With right side facing, join Color B with sl st to any dc, ch 6 (counts as first dc & ch-3), skip next dc, [dc in next dc, ch 3, skip next dc] around; join with sl st to first dc (3rd ch of beg ch-3). (12 dc & 12 ch-3 sps) Fasten off Color B and weave in all ends.

ROUND 3: With right side facing, join Color C with sl st to same st as joining, ch 1 (NOT counted as first st), [3 sc in next ch-3 sp] around; join with sl st to first sc. (36 sc)

Fasten off Color C and weave in all ends.

ROUND 4: With right side facing, join Color D with sl st to any sc, ch 4 (counts as first tr), *wrap yarn twice around hook, insert hook in next st, pull up lp, [yo, draw through 2 lps on hook] 2 times, rep from * once more (3 lps on hook), yo and draw through all 3 lps (first cluster made), ch 5, *3tr-cl (using next 3 sc), ch 5; rep from * around; join with sl st to first tr (4th of beg ch-4). (12 clusters & 12 ch-5 lps)

ROUND 5: Sl st in next ch-5 lp, (3 sc, ch 3, 3 sc) in same lp, *(3 sc, ch 3, 3 sc) in next ch-5 lp; rep from * around; join with sl st to first sc. (72 sc & 12 ch-3 sps) Fasten off Color D and weave in all ends.

Materials
Hook: E-4 (3.50 mm)

DMC Natura Just Cotton:
Color A – N 06 Rose Layette
Color B – N 25 Aguamarina
Color C – N 23 Passion
Color D – N 02 Ivory

Finished Size: 4¾" (13 cm)

3-Treble Cluster (3tr-cl): Wrap yarn twice around hook, insert hook into st or sp indicated, pull up lp (4 lps on hook), [yo, draw through 2 lps on hook] 2 times (2 lps on hook), *wrap yarn twice around hook, insert hook in next st or sp, pull up lp, [yo, draw through 2 lps on hook] 2 times, rep from * once more (4 lps on hook), yo and draw through all 4 lps.

Note: The first Cluster Stitch in a round is started differently to subsequent clusters in round. Instructions for the first cluster are included within the pattern. For subsequent clusters follow the instructions above.

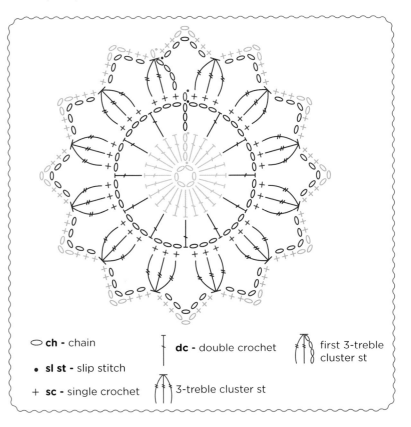

○ **ch -** chain

● **sl st -** slip stitch

+ **sc -** single crochet

| **dc -** double crochet

3-treble cluster st

first 3-treble cluster st

PATTERN

Base Round: Using Color A, ch 4; join with sl st to first ch to form a ring.

ROUND 1: (Right Side) Ch 3 (counts as first dc, now and throughout), 3 dc in ring, ch 5, [4 dc in ring, ch 5] 3 times; join with sl st to first dc (3rd ch of beg ch-3). (16 dc & 4 ch-5 lps)

ROUND 2: Ch 8 (counts as first dc and ch-5, now and throughout), skip next 2 dc, sc in sp before next dc, skip next 2 dc, ch 5, *(2 dc, ch 3, 2 dc) in next ch-5 lp, ch 5, sc in center sp of next 4-dc group, ch 5; rep from * 2 times more, (2 dc, ch 3, dc) in last ch-5 lp; join with sl st to first dc (3rd ch of beg ch-8). (16 dc, 4 sc, 4 ch-3 sps & 8 ch-5 lps)

ROUND 3: Ch 8, [sc in next ch-5 lp, ch 5] 2 times, *(2 dc, ch 3, 2 dc) in next ch-3 sp, ch 5, [sc in next ch-5 lp, ch 5] 2 times; rep from * 2 times more, (2 dc, ch 3, dc) in last ch-3 sp; join with sl st to first dc (3rd ch of beg ch-8). (16 dc, 8 sc, 12 ch-5 lps & 4 ch-3 sps) Fasten off and weave in all ends.

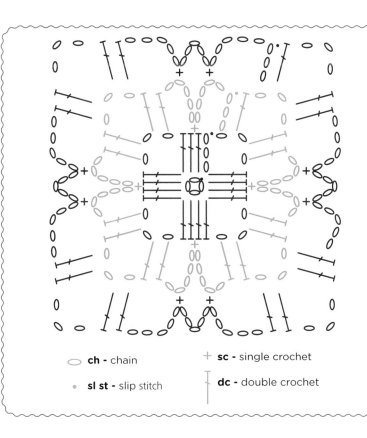

 **ch - chain**

sl st - slip stitch

sc - single crochet

dc - double crochet

Materials
Hook: E-4 (3.50 mm)

DMC Natura Just Cotton:
Color A – N 88 Orléans

Finished Size: 3½" (9 cm)

Motif 31

PATTERN

Base Round: Using Color A, ch 4; join with sl st to first ch to form a ring.

ROUND 1: (Right Side) Ch 1 (NOT counted as first st), 8 sc in ring; join with sl st to first sc. (8 sc)

ROUND 2: Ch 4 (counts as first tr), *wrap yarn twice around hook, insert hook in same st as joining, pull up lp, [yo, draw through 2 lps on hook] 2 times, rep from * once more (4 lps on hook), yo and draw through all 4 lps (first bobble made), ch 5, *4tr-bob in next sc, ch 5; rep from * around; join with sl st to first tr (4th ch of beg ch-4). (8 bobbles & 8 ch-5 lps) Fasten off and weave in all ends.

Materials
Hook: E-4 (3.50 mm)

DMC Natura Just Cotton:
Color A – N 06 Rose Layette

Finished Size: 2¾" (7 cm)

4-Treble Bobble (4tr-bob): Wrap yarn twice around hook, insert hook into st or sp indicated, pull up lp (4 lps on hook), [yo, draw through 2 lps on hook] 2 times (2 lps on hook), *wrap yarn twice around hook, insert hook in same st or sp, pull up lp, [yo, draw through 2 lps on hook] 2 times, rep from * 2 times more (5 lps on hook), yo and draw through all 5 lps.

Note: The first Bobble Stitch in a round is started differently to subsequent bobbles in round. Instructions for the first bobble are included within the pattern. For subsequent bobbles follow the instructions above.

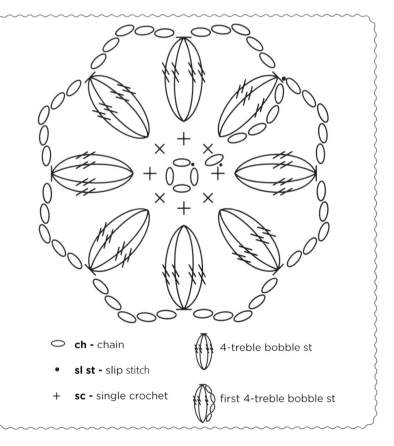

⬭ **ch** - chain	🔶 **4-treble bobble st**
• **sl st** - slip stitch	
+ **sc** - single crochet	🔶 **first 4-treble bobble st**

PATTERN

Base Round: Using Color A, ch 4; join with sl st to first ch to form a ring.

ROUND 1: (Right Side) Ch 4 (counts as first tr), 15 tr in ring; join with sl st to first tr (4th ch of beg ch-4). (16 tr) Fasten off Color A and weave in all ends.

ROUND 2: With right side facing, join Color B with sl st to any tr, ch 5 (counts as first dc & ch-2), [dc in next tr, ch 2] around; join with sl st to first dc (3rd ch of beg ch-5). (16 dc & 16 ch-2 sps) Fasten off Color B and weave in all ends.

ROUND 3: With right side facing, join Color C with sl st to any ch-2 sp, ch 3 (counts as first dc, now and throughout), [yo, insert hook in same sp, pull up lp, yo, draw through 2 lps on hook] 3 times (4 lps on hook), yo, draw through all 4 lps (first 4-bob made), ch 3; [4-bob in next ch-2 sp, ch 3] around; join with sl st to first dc (3rd ch of beg ch-3). (16 bobbles & 16 ch-3 sps) Fasten off Color C and weave in all ends.

ROUND 4: With right side facing, join Color D with sl st to any ch-3 sp, ch 3, 2 dc in same sp, 3 dc in next ch-3 sp, ch 3, *[3 dc in next ch-3 sp] 2 times, ch 3; rep from * around; join with sl st to first dc (3rd ch of beg ch-3). (48 dc & 8 ch-3 sps) Fasten off Color D and weave in all ends.

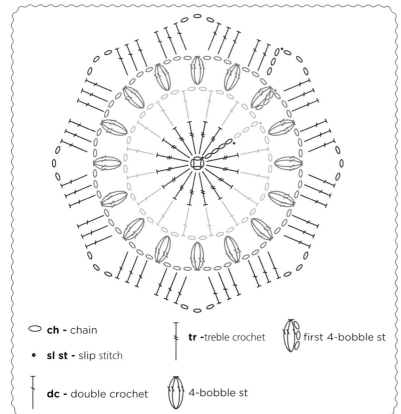

◯ **ch -** chain

• **sl st -** slip stitch

dc - double crochet

tr - treble crochet

first 4-bobble st

4-bobble st

Materials
Hook: E-4 (3.50 mm)

DMC Natura Just Cotton:
Color A – N 79 Tilleul
Color B – N 75 Moss Green
Color C – N 76 Bamboo
Color D – N 31 Malva

Finished Size: 4¾" (12 cm)

4-Bobble Stitch (4-bob): Yo, insert hook into st or sp indicated, pull up lp, yo, draw through 2 lps on hook, [yo, insert hook in same st or sp, pull up lp, yo, draw through 2 lps on hook] 3 times more (5 lps on hook), yo and draw through all 5 lps.

Note: The first Bobble Stitch in a round is started differently to subsequent bobbles in round. Instructions for the first bobble are included within the pattern. For subsequent bobbles follow the instructions above.

Motif 33

PATTERN

Base Round: Using Color A, ch 4; join with sl st to first ch to form a ring.

ROUND 1: (Right Side) Ch 8 (counts as first dc & ch-5), [dc in ring, ch 5] 7 times; join with sl st to first dc (3rd ch of beg ch-8). (8 dc & ch-5 lps) Fasten off Color A and weave in all ends.

ROUND 2: With right side facing, using Color B, join with sc to any ch-5 lp, (hdc, 2 dc, ch 1, 2 dc, hdc, sc) in same lp, *(sc, hdc, 2 dc, ch 1, 2 dc, hdc, sc) in next ch-5 lp; rep from * around; join with sl st to first sc. (8 petals) Fasten off Color B and weave in all ends.

ROUND 3: With right side facing, join Color C with sl st to any ch-1 sp, ch 1 (NOT counted as first st, now and throughout), sc in same sp, ch 6, [sc in next ch-1 sp, ch 6] around; join with sl st to first sc. (8 sc & 8 ch-6 lps)

ROUND 4: Sl st in next ch-6 lp, ch 1, 4 sc in same lp, ch 3, (3-bob, ch 5, 3-bob) in next ch-6 lp, ch 3, *4 sc in next lp, ch 3, (3-bob, ch 5, 3-bob) in next lp, ch 3; rep from * around; join with sl st to first sc. (8 bobbles, 16 sc, 8 ch-3 sps & 4 ch-5 lps) Fasten off Color C and weave in all ends.

Materials

Hook: E-4 (3.50 mm)

DMC Natura Just Cotton:
Color A – N 06 Rose Layette
Color B – N 03 Sable
Color C – N 38 Liquen

Finished Size: 3½" (9 cm)

3-Bobble Stitch (3-bob): Yo, insert hook into st or sp indicated, pull up lp, yo, draw through 2 lps on hook, [yo, insert hook in same st or sp, pull up lp, yo, draw through 2 lps on hook] 2 times more (4 lps on hook), yo and draw through all 4 lps.

Join with Single Crochet: With slip knot on hook, insert hook in st or sp indicated, pull up lp (2 lps on hook), yo, draw through both loops on hook (first single crochet made).

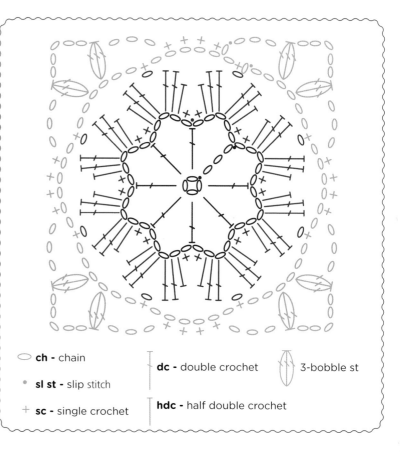

◯ **ch -** chain	│ **dc -** double crochet	◯ **3-bobble st**
• **sl st -** slip stitch		
+ **sc -** single crochet	│ **hdc -** half double crochet	

PATTERN

Base Round: Using Color A, ch 5; join with sl st to first ch to form a ring.

ROUND 1: (Right Side) Ch 4 (counts as first tr), 23 tr in ring; join with sl st to first tr (4th ch of beg ch-4). (24 tr)

ROUND 2: Ch 3 (counts as first dc), dc in next 2 sts, ch 2, * dc in next 3 sts, ch 2. Repeat from * to end. Join with a sl st into top of first ch-3.

ROUND 3: Ch 3, dc in each of next 2 dc, ch 3, *dc in each of next 3 dc, ch 3; rep from * around; join with sl st to first dc. (24 dc & 8 ch-3 sps)

ROUND 4: Ch 3, [yo, insert hook in next dc, pull up lp, yo, draw through 2 lps on hook] 2 times (3 lps on hook), yo and draw through all 3 lps (first cluster made), ch 5, sc in next ch-3 sp, ch 5, *3dc-cl (using next 3 dc), ch 5, sc in next sp, ch 5; rep from * around; join with sl st to first dc. (8 clusters, 8 sc & 16 ch-5 lps) Fasten off and weave in all ends.

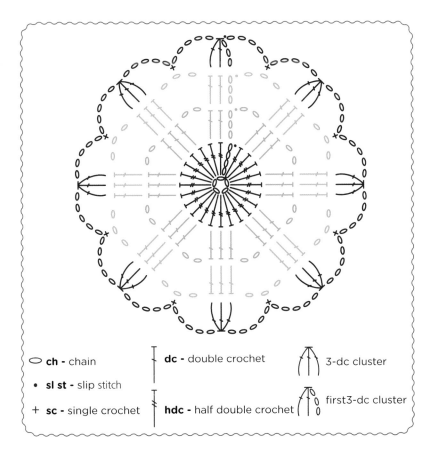

⌒ **ch -** chain

• **sl st -** slip stitch

+ **sc -** single crochet

dc - double crochet

hdc - half double crochet

3-dc cluster

first 3-dc cluster

Materials
Hook: E-4 (3.50 mm)

DMC Natura Just Cotton:
Color A – N 03 Sable

Finished Size: 4¼" (11 cm)

3-Double Crochet Cluster (3dc-cl): Yo, insert hook into st or sp indicated, pull up lp (3 lps on hook), yo, draw through 2 lps on hook (2 lps on hook), *yo, insert hook in next st or sp, pull up lp, yo, draw through 2 lps on hook; rep from * once more (4 lps on hook), yo and draw through all 4 lps.

Note: The first Cluster Stitch in a round is started differently to subsequent clusters in round. Instructions for the first cluster are included within the pattern. For subsequent clusters follow the instructions above.

Materials

Hook: E-4 (3.50 mm)

DMC Natura Just Cotton:
Color A – N 26 Blue Jeans

Finished Size: 4¾" (12 cm)

2-Treble Bobble (2tr-bob): Wrap yarn twice around hook, insert hook into st or sp indicated, pull up lp (4 lps on hook), [yo, draw through 2 lps on hook] 2 times (2 lps on hook), wrap yarn twice around hook, insert hook in same st or sp, pull up lp, [yo, draw through 2 lps on hook] 2 times (3 lps on hook), yo and draw through all 3 lps.

3-Treble Bobble (3tr-bob): Wrap yarn twice around hook, insert hook into st or sp indicated, pull up lp (4 lps on hook), [yo, draw through 2 lps on hook] 2 times (2 lps on hook), *wrap yarn twice around hook, insert hook in same st or sp, pull up lp, [yo, draw through 2 lps on hook] 2 times, rep from * once more (4 lps on hook), yo and draw through all 4 lps.

Note: The first Bobble Stitch in a round is started differently to subsequent bobbles in round. Instructions for the first bobble are included within the pattern. For subsequent bobbles follow the instructions above.

PATTERN

Base Round: Using Color A, ch 4; join with sl st to first ch to form a ring.

ROUND 1: (Right Side) Ch 4 (counts as first tr, now and throughout), wrap yarn twice around hook, insert hook in ring, pull up lp, [yo, draw through 2 lps on hook] 2 times (2 lps on hook), yo and draw through both lps (first 2tr-bob made) ch 3, [2tr-bob in ring, ch 3] 5 times; join with sl st to first tr (4th ch of beg ch-4). (6 bobbles & 6 ch-3 sps)

ROUND 2: Sl st in next ch-3 sp, ch 1 (NOT counted as first st), 3 sc in same sp, ch 3, [3 sc in next sp, ch 3] around; join with sl st to first sc. (18 sc & 6 ch-3 sps)

ROUND 3: Sl st in each of next 3 sc, sl st in next ch-3 sp, ch 4, wrap yarn twice around hook, insert hook in same sp, pull up lp, [yo, draw through 2 lps on hook] 2 times (2 lps on hook), yo and draw through both lps (first 2tr-bob made), ch 3, 2tr-bob in same sp, ch 3, *(2tr-bob, ch 3, 2tr-bob) in next sp, ch 3; rep from * around; join with sl st to first tr (4th ch of beg ch-4). (12 bobbles & 12 ch-3 sps)

ROUND 4: Sl st in next ch-3 sp, ch 4, wrap yarn twice around hook, insert hook in same sp, pull up lp, [yo, draw through 2 lps on hook] 2 times (2 lps on hook), wrap yarn twice around hook, insert hook in same sp, pull up lp, [yo, draw through 2 lps on hook] 2 times (2 lps on hook), yo and draw through 3 lps (first 3tr-bob made), ch 3, 3tr-bob in same sp, ch 3, sc in next ch-3 sp, ch 3, *(3tr-bob, ch 3, 3tr-bob) in next sp, ch 3, sc in next sp, ch 3; rep from * around; join with sl st to first tr (4th ch of beg ch-4). (12 bobbles, 6 sc & 18 ch-3 sps) Fasten off and weave in all ends.

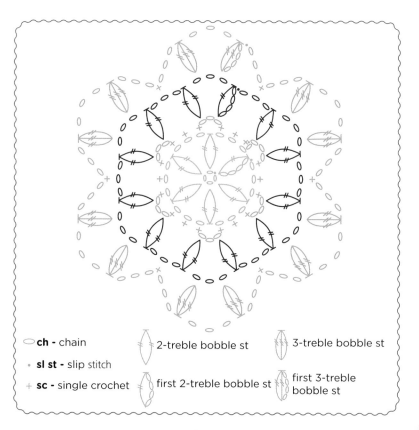

⌒ **ch** - chain

∙ **sl st** - slip stitch

+ **sc** - single crochet

2-treble bobble st

first 2-treble bobble st

3-treble bobble st

first 3-treble bobble st

PATTERN

Base Round: Using Color A, ch 4; join with sl st to first ch to form a ring.

ROUND 1: (Right Side) Ch 1 (NOT counted as first st, now and throughout), 12 sc in ring; join with sl st to first sc. (12 sc)

ROUND 2: Ch 3 (counts as first dc, now and throughout), yo, insert hook in same st as joining, pull up lp, yo, draw through 2 lps on hook (2 lps on hook), yo and draw through all lps (first 2-bob made), ch 2, [2-bob in next sc, ch 2] around; join with sl st to first dc (3rd ch of beg ch-3). (12 bobbles & 12 ch-2 sps)

ROUND 3: Sl st in next ch-2 sp, ch 1, sc in same sp, ch 5, [sc in next sp, ch 5] around; join with sl st to first sc. (12 sc & 12 ch-5 lps)

ROUND 4: Sl st in next ch-5 lp, ch 1, (sc, ch 7 sc) in same lp, ch 5, dc in next lp, ch 5, *(sc, ch 7, sc) in next lp, ch 5, dc in next lp, ch 5; rep from * around; join with sl st to first sc. (12 sc, 6 dc, 6 ch-7 lps & 12 ch-5 lps)

ROUND5: Sl st in next ch-7 lp, ch 3, (4 dc, ch 3, 5 dc) in same lp, 2 sc in next ch-5 lp, ch 1, 2 sc in next ch-5 lp, *(5 dc, ch 3, 5 dc) in next ch-7 lp, 2 sc in next lp, ch 1, 2 sc in next lp; rep from * around; join with sl st to first dc (3rd ch of beg ch-3). (60 dc, 6 ch-3 sps, 24 sc & 6 ch-1 sps)

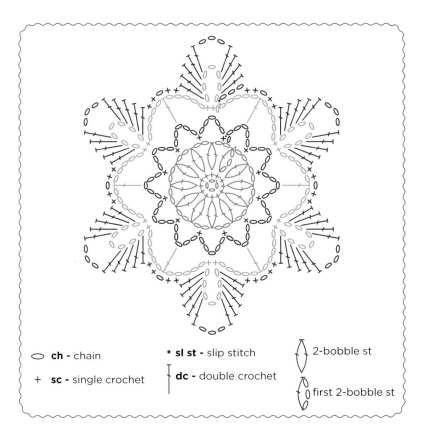

⬭ **ch -** chain	• **sl st -** slip stitch
+ **sc -** single crochet	┃ **dc -** double crochet

2-bobble st

first 2-bobble st

Materials
Hook: E-4 (3.50 mm)

DMC Natura Just Cotton:
Color A – N 03 Sable

Finished Size: 5¼″ (14 cm)

2-Bobble Stitch (2-bob): Yo, insert hook into st or sp indicated, pull up lp, yo, draw through 2 lps on hook, yo, insert hook in same st or sp, pull up lp, yo, draw through 2 lps on hook (3 lps on hook), yo and draw through all 3 lps.

Note: The first Bobble Stitch in a round is started differently to subsequent bobbles in round. Instructions for the first bobble are included within the pattern. For subsequent bobbles follow the instructions above.

Motif 37

PATTERN

Base Round: Using Color A, ch 4; join with sl st to first ch to form a ring.

ROUND 1: (Right Side) Ch 1 (NOT counted as first st, now and throughout), 8 sc in ring; join with sl st to first sc. (8 sc)

ROUND 2: Ch 1, (sc, ch 11, sc) in same st as joining, skip next sc, *(sc, ch 11, sc) in next sc, skip next sc; rep from * around; join with sl st to first sc. (8 sc & 4 ch-11 lps)

ROUND 3: Sl st in next ch-11 sp, ch 1, (5 sc, ch 2, 5 sc) in same lp, *(5 sc, ch 2, 5 sc) in next lp; rep from * around; join with sl st to first sc. (40 sc & 4 ch-2 sps)

ROUND 4: Ch 6 (counts as first dc & ch-3), dc in same st as joining, ch 7, (3 dc, ch 3, 3 dc) in next ch-2 sp, ch 7, *(dc, ch 3, dc) in sp between petals, ch 7, (3 dc, ch 3, 3 dc) in next ch-2 sp, ch 7; rep from * around; join with sl st to first dc (3rd ch of beg ch-6). (32 dc, 8 ch-3 sps, & 8 ch-7 lps)

Materials
Hook: E-4 (3.50 mm)

DMC Natura Just Cotton:
Color A – N 38 Liquen

Finished Size: 3¼" (8 cm)

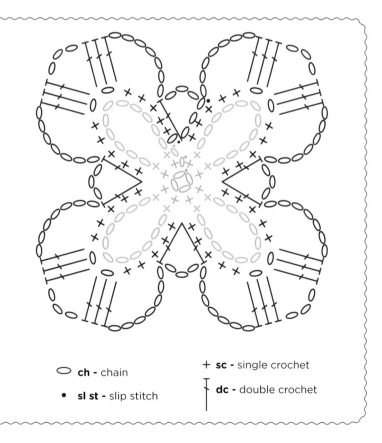

◯ **ch -** chain

• **sl st -** slip stitch

+ **sc -** single crochet

┆ **dc -** double crochet

PATTERN

Base Round: Using Color A, ch 4; join with sl st to first ch to form a ring.

ROUND 1: (Right Side) Ch 3 (counts as first dc, now and throughout), [yo, insert hook in ring, pull up lp, yo, draw through 2 lps on hook] 2 times (3 lps on hook), yo and draw through all 3 lps (first 3-bob made), ch 3, [3-bob in ring, ch 3] 5 times; join with sl st to first dc (3rd ch of beg ch-3). (6 bobbles & 6 ch-3 sps)

ROUND 2: Sl st in next ch-3 sp, ch 3, [yo, insert hook in same sp, pull up lp, yo, draw through 2 lps on hook] 2 times (3 lps on hook), yo and draw through all 3 lps (first 3-bob made), ch 3, 3-bob in same sp, ch 3, 3-bob in next sp, ch 3, *(3-bob, ch 3, 3-bob) in next ch-3 sp, ch 3, 3-bob in next sp, ch 3; rep from * around; join with sl st to first dc (3rd ch of beg ch-3). (9 bobbles & 9 ch-3 sps)

ROUND 3: Sl st in next ch-3 sp, [yo, insert hook in same sp, pull up lp, yo, draw through 2 lps on hook] 2 times (3 lps on hook), yo and draw through all 3 lps (first 3-bob made), ch 3, 3-bob in same sp, ch 5, [sc in next sp, ch 5] 2 times, *(3-bob, ch 3, 3-bob) in next sp, ch 5, [sc in next sp, ch 5] 2 times; rep from * around; join with sl st to first dc (3rd ch of beg ch-3). (6 bobbles, 3 ch-3 sps, 6 sc & 9 ch-5 lps)

ROUND 4: Sl st in next ch-3 sp, [yo, insert hook in same sp, pull up lp, yo, draw through 2 lps on hook] 2 times (3 lps on hook), yo and draw through all 3 lps (first 3-bob made), ch 3, 3-bob in same sp, ch 5, [sc in next sp, ch 5] 3 times, *(3-bob, ch 3, 3-bob) in next sp, ch 5, [sc in next sp, ch 5] 3 times; rep from * around; join with sl st to first dc (3rd ch of beg ch-3). (6 bobbles, 3 ch-3 sps, 9 sc & 12 ch-5 lps) Fasten off and weave in all ends.

Materials
Hook: E-4 (3.50 mm)

DMC Natura Just Cotton:
Color A – N 80 Salomé

Finished Size: 4¼" (12 cm)

3-Bobble Stitch (3-bob): Yo, insert hook into st or sp indicated, pull up lp, yo, draw through 2 lps on hook, [yo, insert hook in same st or sp, pull up lp, yo, draw through 2 lps on hook] 2 times more (4 lps on hook), yo and draw through all 4 lps.

Note: The first Bobble Stitch in a round is started differently to subsequent bobbles in round. Instructions for the first bobble are included within the pattern. For subsequent bobbles follow the instructions above.

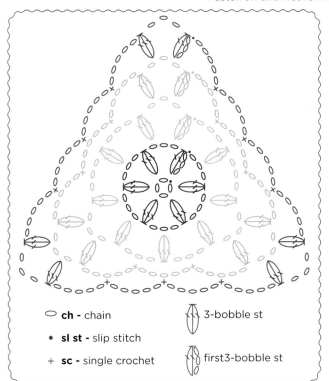

⬭ **ch -** chain	⬭ 3-bobble st
• **sl st -** slip stitch	first3-bobble st
+ **sc -** single crochet	

Motif 39

Materials
Hook: E-4 (3.50 mm)

DMC Natura Just Cotton:
Color A – N 34 Bourgogne
Color B – N 09 Gris Argent

Finished Size: 4¾" (12 cm)

3-Bobble Stitch (3-bob): Yo, insert hook into st or sp indicated, pull up lp, yo, draw through 2 lps on hook, [yo, insert hook in same st or sp, pull up lp, yo, draw through 2 lps on hook] 2 times more (4 lps on hook), yo and draw through all 4 lps.

2-Treble Bobble (2tr-bob): Wrap yarn twice around hook, insert hook into st or sp indicated, pull up lp (4 lps on hook), [yo, draw through 2 lps on hook] 2 times (2 lps on hook), wrap yarn twice around hook, insert hook in same st or sp, pull up lp, [yo, draw through 2 lps on hook] 2 times (3 lps on hook), yo and draw through all 3 lps.

3-Treble Bobble (3tr-bob): Wrap yarn twice around hook, insert hook into st or sp indicated, pull up lp (4 lps on hook), [yo, draw through 2 lps on hook] 2 times (2 lps on hook), *wrap yarn twice around hook, insert hook in same st or sp, pull up lp, [yo, draw through 2 lps on hook] 2 times, rep from * once more (4 lps on hook), yo and draw through all 4 lps

Note: The first Bobble Stitch in a round is started differently to subsequent bobbles in round. Instructions for the first bobble are included within the pattern. For subsequent bobbles follow the instructions above.

Pattern:

Base Round: Using Color A, ch 4; join with sl st to first ch to form a ring.

ROUND 1: (Right Side) Ch 4 (counts as first tr, now and throughout), wrap yarn twice around hook, insert hook in ring, pull up lp, [yo, draw through 2 lps on hook] 2 times (2 lps on hook), yo and draw through both lps (first 2tr-bob made) ch 3, 2tr-bob in ring, ch 5, *(2tr-bob, ch 3, 2tr-bob) in ring, ch 5; rep from * once more; join with sl st to first tr (4th ch of beg ch-4). (6 bobbles, 3 ch-3 sps & 3 ch-5 lps)

ROUND 2: Ch 6 (counts as first dc & ch-3), sc in next ch-3 sp, ch 3, *(3 sc, ch 5, 3 dc) in next ch-5 lp, ch 3, sc in next ch-3 sp, ch 3; rep from * once more, (3 sc, ch 5, 2 dc) in last lp; join with sl st to first dc (3rd ch of beg ch-6). (18 dc, 3 ch-5 lps, 3 sc & 6 ch-3 sps) Fasten off Color A and weave in all ends.

ROUND 3: With right side facing, join Color B with sl st to any ch-5 lp, ch 4, *wrap yarn twice around hook, insert hook in same lp, pull up lp, [yo, draw through 2 lps on hook] 2 times, rep from * once more (3 lps on hook), yo and draw through all 3 lps (first bobble made), ch 5, 3tr-bob in same lp, ch 5, 3 dc in next ch-3 sp, ch 1, 3 dc in next ch-3 sp, ch 5, *(3tr-bob, ch 5, 3tr-bob in next ch-5 lp, ch 5, 3 dc in next ch-3 sp, ch 1, 3 dc in next ch-3 sp, ch 5; rep from * around; join with sl st to first tr (4th ch of beg ch-4) (6 bobbles, 18 dc, 3 ch-1 sps & 9 ch-5 lps)

ROUND 4: Sl st in next ch-5 lp, ch 3 (counts as first dc), [yo, insert hook in same lp, pull up lp, yo, draw through 2 lps on hook] 2 times (3 lps on hook), yo and draw through all 3 lps (first 3-bob made), ch 5, 3-bob in same lp, ch 5, sc in next ch-5 lp, ch 5, sc in next ch-1 sp, ch 5, sc in next ch-5 lp, ch 5, *(3-bob, ch 5, 3-bob) in next lp, ch 5, sc in next ch-5 lp, ch 5, sc in next ch-1 sp, ch 5, sc in next ch-5 lp, ch 5; rep from * around; join with sl st to first dc (3rd ch of beg ch-3). (6 bobbles, 9 sc & 15 ch-5 lps) Fasten off Color B and weave in all ends.

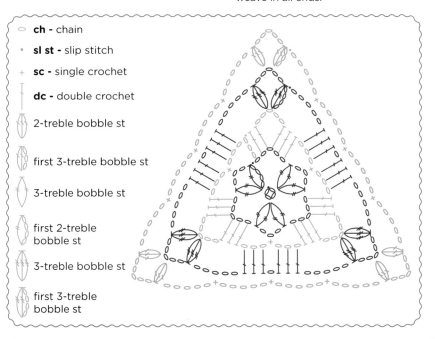

- ⊖ **ch -** chain
- • **sl st -** slip stitch
- + **sc -** single crochet
- | **dc -** double crochet
- 2-treble bobble st
- first 3-treble bobble st
- 3-treble bobble st
- first 2-treble bobble st
- 3-treble bobble st
- first 3-treble bobble st

Pattern:

Base Round: Using Color A, ch 4; join with sl st to first ch to form a ring.

ROUND 1: (Right Side) Ch 3 (counts as first dc, now and throughout), yo, insert hook in ring, pull up lp, yo, draw through 2 lps on hook (2 lps on hook), yo and draw through all lps (first 2-bob made), ch 3, [2-bob in ring, ch 3] 5 times; join with sl st to first dc (3rd ch of beg ch-3). (6 bobbles & 6 ch-3 sps) Fasten off and weave in all ends.

ROUND 2: With right side facing, join Color B with sl st to any ch-3 sp, ch 3, 2 dc in same sp, ch 3, [3 dc in next sp, ch 3] around; join with sl st to first dc (3rd ch of beg ch-3). (18 dc & 6 ch-3 sps) Fasten off Color B and weave in all ends.

ROUND 3: With right side facing, join Color C with sl st to any ch-3 sp, ch 4 (counts as first dc & ch-1, now and throughout), (dc, ch 1, dc, ch 3, dc, [ch 1, dc] 2 times) in same sp, ch 1, skip next dc, sc in next (center) dc, ch 1, skip next dc, *([dc, ch 1] 2 times, dc, ch 3, dc, [ch 1, dc] 2 times) in next ch-3 sp, ch 1, skip next dc, sc in next (center) dc, ch 1, skip next dc; rep from * around; join with sl st to first dc (3rd ch of beg ch-4). (6 petals) Fasten off Color C and weave in all ends.

ROUND 4: With right side facing, join Color D with sl st in any ch-3 sp, ch 4, (dc, ch 1, dc, ch 3, dc, [ch 1, dc] 2 times) in same sp, ch 2, sc in next sc, ch 2, *([dc, ch 1] 2 times, dc, ch 3, dc, [ch 1, dc] 2 times) in next ch-3 sp, ch 2, sc in next sc, ch 2; rep from * around; join with sl st to first dc (3rd ch of beg ch-4). (6 petals) Fasten off Color D and weave in all ends.

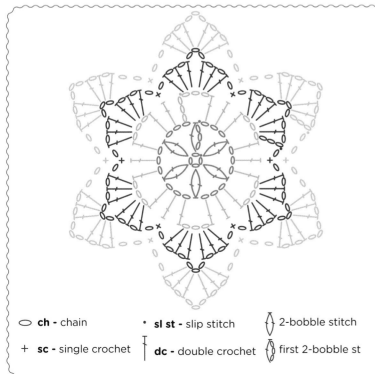

◠ **ch** - chain

╺ **sl st** - slip stitch

◇ **2-bobble stitch**

+ **sc** - single crochet

丅 **dc** - double crochet

⬧ **first 2-bobble st**

Materials
Hook: E-4 (3.50 mm)

DMC Natura Just Cotton:
Color A – N 30 Glicine
Color B – N 05 Bleu Layette
Color C – N 85 Giroflée
Color D – N 76 Bamboo

Finished Size: 4¾" (12 cm)

2-Bobble Stitch (2-bob): Yo, insert hook into st or sp indicated, pull up lp, yo, draw through 2 lps on hook, yo, insert hook in same st or sp, pull up lp, yo, draw through 2 lps on hook (3 lps on hook), yo and draw through all 3 lps.

Note: The first Bobble Stitch in a round is started differently to subsequent bobbles in round. Instructions for the first bobble are included within the pattern. For subsequent bobbles follow the directions above.

Motif 41

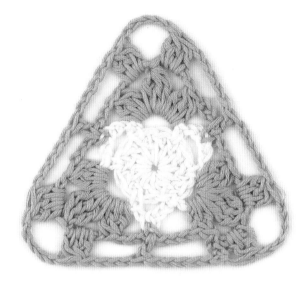

Materials
Hook: E-4 (3.50 mm)

DMC Natura Just Cotton:
Color A – N 79 Tilleul
Color B – N 44 Agatha

Finished Size: 4″ (10 cm)

3-Bobble Stitch (3-bob): Yo, insert hook into st or sp indicated, pull up lp, yo, draw through 2 lps on hook, [yo, insert hook in same st or sp, pull up lp, yo, draw through 2 lps on hook] 2 times more (4 lps on hook), yo and draw through all 4 lps.

3-Treble Bobble (3tr-bob): Wrap yarn twice around hook, insert hook into st or sp indicated, pull up lp (4 lps on hook), [yo, draw through 2 lps on hook] 2 times (2 lps on hook), *wrap yarn twice around hook, insert hook in same st or sp, pull up lp, [yo, draw through 2 lps on hook] 2 times, rep from * once more (4 lps on hook), yo and draw through all 4 lps.

Note: The first Bobble Stitch in a round is started differently to subsequent bobbles in round. Instructions for the first bobble are included within the pattern. For subsequent bobbles follow the instructions above.

PATTERN

Base Round: Using Color A, ch 4; join with sl st to first ch to form a ring.

ROUND 1: (Right Side) Ch 3 (counts as first dc, now and throughout), 11 dc in ring; join with sl st to first dc (3rd ch of beg ch-3). (12 dc)

ROUND 2: Ch 1 (NOT counted as first st), sc in same st as joining, ch 5, skip next dc, *sc in next dc, ch 5, skip next dc; rep from * around; join with sl st to first sc. (6 sc & 6 ch-5 lps) Fasten off Color A and weave in all ends.

ROUND 3: With right side facing, join Color B with sl st to any ch-5 lp, ch 3, [yo, insert hook in same lp, pull up lp, yo, draw through 2 lps on hook] 2 times (3 lps on hook), yo and draw through all 3 lps (first 3-bob made), ch 4, (3tr-bob, ch 4, 3-bob) in same lp, ch 3, sc in next ch-5 lp, ch 3, *(3-bob, ch 4, 3tr-bob, ch 4, 3-bob) in next lp, ch 3, sc in next ch-5 lp, ch 3; rep from * around; join with sl st to first dc (3rd ch of beg ch-3). (6 bobbles, 3 tr-bobbles, 3 sc, 6 ch-3 sps & 6 ch-4 lps)

ROUND 4: Sl st in next ch-4 sp, ch 3, [yo, insert hook in same lp, pull up lp, yo, draw through 2 lps on hook] 2 times (3 lps on hook), yo and draw through all 3 lps (first 3-bob made), ch 5, 3-bob in next ch-4 lp, ch 5, dc in next sc, ch 5, *[3-bob in next ch-4 lp, ch 5] 2 times, dc in next sc, ch 5; rep from * around; join with sl st to first dc (3rd ch of beg ch-3). (6 bobbles & 9 ch-5 lps) Fasten off Color B and weave in all ends.

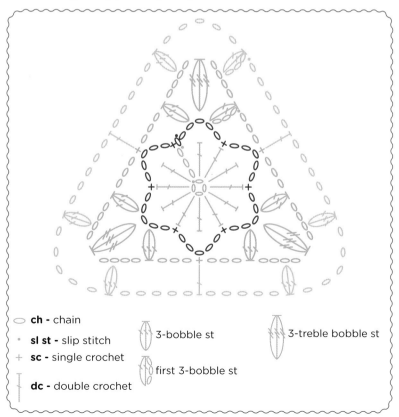

⬭ **ch** - chain

· **sl st** - slip stitch

+ **sc** - single crochet

╎ **dc** - double crochet

〜 **3-bobble st**

〜 **first 3-bobble st**

〜 **3-treble bobble st**

PATTERN

Base Round: Using Color A, ch 4; join with sl st to first ch to form a ring.

ROUND 1: (Right Side) Ch 1 (NOT counted as first st), 6 sc in ring; join with sl st to first sc. (6 sc)

ROUND 2: Ch 3 (counts as first dc, now and throughout), [yo, insert hook in same st as joining, pull up lp, yo, draw through 2 lps on hook] 2 times (3 lps on hook), yo and draw through all 3 lps (first 3-bob made), ch 5, *3-bob in next sc, ch 5; 3-bob in next sc, ch 3; rep from * around; join with sl st to first dc (3rd ch of beg ch-3). (6 bobbles & 6 ch-5 lps) Fasten off Color A and weave in all ends.

ROUND 3: With right side facing, join Color B with sl st to any ch-5 lp, ch 3, [yo, insert hook in same ch-5 lp, pull up lp, yo, draw through 2 lps on hook] 2 times (3 lps on hook), yo and draw through all 3 lps (first 3-bob made), ch 3, (dtr, ch 3, 3-bob) in same lp, ch 3, sc in next ch-5 lp, ch 3, *(3-bob, ch 3, dtr, ch 3, 3-bob) in next lp, ch 3, sc in next lp, ch 3; rep from * around; join with sl st to first dc (3rd ch of beg ch-3). (6 bobbles, 3 dtr & 12 ch-3 sps) Fasten off Color B and weave in all ends.

ROUND 4: With right side facing, join Color C with sl st to first ch-3 sp (before tr), ch 3, 2 dc in same sp, *ch 3, 3 dc in next sp, [ch 1, 3 dc in next sp] 3 times; rep from * once more, ch 3, 3 dc in next sp, [ch 1, 3 dc in next sp] 2 times, ch 1; join with sl st to first dc (3rd ch of beg ch-3). (36 dc, 3 ch-3 sps & 9 ch-1 sps) Fasten off Color C and weave in all ends.

Materials
Hook: E-4 (3.50 mm)

DMC Natura Just Cotton:
Color A – N 83 Blé
Color B – N 76 Bamboo
Color C – N 85 Giroflée

Finished Size: 4″ (10 cm)

3-Bobble Stitch (3-bob): Yo, insert hook into st or sp indicated, pull up lp, yo, draw through 2 lps on hook, [yo, insert hook in same st or sp, pull up lp, yo, draw through 2 lps on hook] 2 times more (4 lps on hook), yo and draw through all 4 lps.

Note: The first Bobble Stitch in a round is started differently to subsequent bobbles in round. Instructions for the first bobble are included within the pattern. For subsequent bobbles follow the instructions above.

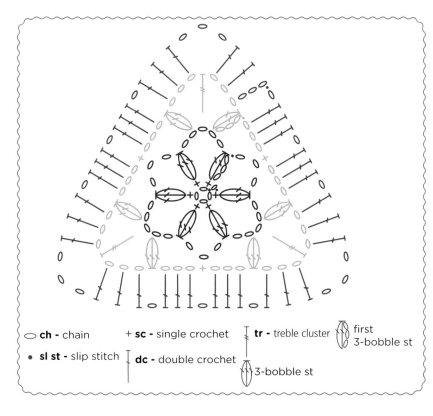

⬯ **ch** - chain   + **sc** - single crochet   **tr** - treble cluster   first 3-bobble st

• **sl st** - slip stitch   **dc** - double crochet   3-bobble st

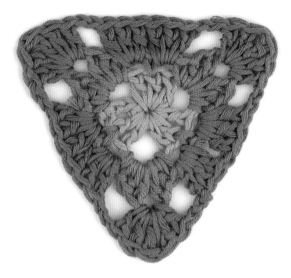

PATTERN

Base Round: Using Color A, ch 4; join with sl st to first ch to form a ring.

ROUND 1: (Right Side) Ch 3 (counts as first dc, now and throughout), 2 dc in ring, ch 3, [3 dc in ring, ch 3] 2 times; join with sl st to first dc (3rd ch of beg ch-3). (9 dc & 3 ch-3 sps) Fasten off Color A and weave in all ends.

ROUND 2: With right side facing, join Color B with sl st in center dc of any 3-dc group, ch 1 (NOT counted as first st), sc in same dc, ch 3, (sc, hdc, dc, ch 3, dc, hdc, sc) in next ch-3 sp, ch 3, * sc in center dc of next 3-dc group, ch 3, (sc, hdc, dc, ch 3, dc, hdc, sc) in next ch-3 sp, ch 3; join with sl st to first sc. (3 petals, 3 sc & 6 ch-3 sps) Fasten off and weave in all ends.

ROUND 3: With right side facing, join Color C with sl st to last ch-3 sp (before single sc), ch 3, 2 dc in same sp, 3 dc in next ch-3 sp, ch 2, (2 dc, tr, 2 dc) in next sp, ch 2, *3 dc in each of next 2 ch-3 sps, ch 2, (2 dc, tr, 2 dc) in next sp, ch 2; rep from * around; join with sl st to first dc (3rd ch of beg ch-3). (30 dc, 3 tr, & 6 ch-2 sps) Fasten off and weave in all ends.

Materials
Hook: E-4 (3.50 mm)

DMC Natura Just Cotton:
Color A – N 25 Aguamarina
Color B – N 31 Malva
Color C –N 26 Blue Jeans

Finished Size: 4″ (10 cm)

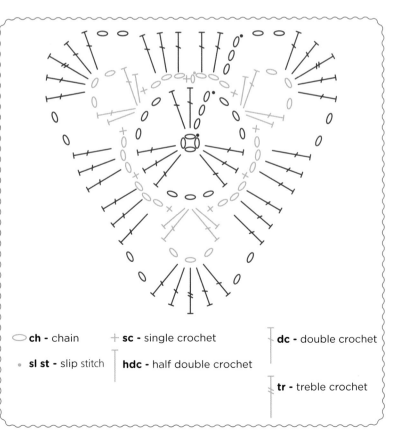

⬭ **ch - chain**   ＋ **sc - single crochet**   **dc - double crochet**

• **sl st - slip stitch**   **hdc - half double crochet**

tr - treble crochet

PATTERN

Base Round: Using Color A, ch 4; join with sl st to first ch to form a ring.

ROUND 1: (Right Side) Ch 4 (counts as first tr), wrap yarn twice around hook, insert hook in ring, pull up lp, [yo, draw through 2 lps on hook] 2 times (2 lps on hook), yo and draw through both lps (first 2tr-bob made) ch 3, [2tr-bob in ring, ch 3] 5 times; join with sl st to first tr (4th ch of beg ch-4). (6 bobbles & 6 ch-3 sps) Fasten off Color A and weave in all ends.

ROUND 2: With right side facing, join Color B with sl st to any ch-3 sp, ch 1 (NOT counted as first st), sc in same sp, ch 7, sc in next ch-3 sp, ch 5, *sc in next sp, ch 7, sc in next sp, ch 5; rep from * around; join with sl st to first sc. (6 sc, 3 ch-7 lps & 3 ch-5 lps) Fasten off Color B and weave in all ends.

ROUND 3: With right side facing, join Color C with sl st to any ch-7 lp, ch 3 (counts as first dc), yo, insert hook in same ch-7 lp, pull up lp, yo, draw through 2 lps on hook (2 lps on hook), yo and draw through all lps (first 2-bob made), ch 1, (2-bob, ch 5, 2-bob, ch 1, 2-bob) in same sp, ch 3, sc in next ch-5 lp, ch 3, *(2-bob, ch 1, 2-bob, ch 5, 2-bob, ch 1, 2-bob) in same sp, ch 3, sc in next ch-5 lp, ch 3; rep from * around; join with sl st to first dc (3rd ch of beg ch-3). (12 bobbles, 3 sc, 6 ch-1 sp, 3 ch-5 lps & 6 ch-2 sps) Fasten off Color C and weave in all ends.

⬯ **ch -** chain

+ **sl st -** slip stitch

. **sc -** single crochet

⬙ 2-bobble st

⬙ first 2-bobble st

⬙ 2-treble bobble st

⬙ first 2-treble bobble st

Materials
Hook: E-4 (3.50 mm)

DMC Natura Just Cotton:
Color A – N 25 Aguamarina
Color B – N 43 Golden Lemon
Color C – N 05 Bleu Layette

Finished Size: 4″ (10 cm)

2-Bobble Stitch (2-bob): Yo, insert hook into st or sp indicated, pull up lp, yo, draw through 2 lps on hook, yo, insert hook in same st or sp, pull up lp, yo, draw through 2 lps on hook (3 lps on hook), yo and draw through all 3 lps.

2-Treble Bobble (2tr-bob): Wrap yarn twice around hook, insert hook into st or sp indicated, pull up lp (4 lps on hook), [yo, draw through 2 lps on hook] 2 times (2 lps on hook), wrap yarn twice around hook, insert hook in same st or sp, pull up lp, [yo, draw through 2 lps on hook] 2 times (3 lps on hook), yo and draw through all 3 lps.

Note: The first Bobble Stitch in a round is started differently to subsequent bobbles in round. Instructions for the first bobble are included within the pattern. For subsequent bobbles follow the instructions above.

Motif 45

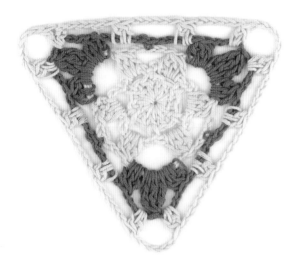

Materials
Hook: E-4 (3.50 mm)

DMC Natura Just Cotton:
Color A – N 06 Rose Layette
Color B – N 43 Golden Lemon
Color C – N 31 Malva
Color D – N 79 Tilleul

Finished Size: 5½" (14 cm)

2-Bobble Stitch (2-bob): Yo, insert hook into st or sp indicated, pull up lp, yo, draw through 2 lps on hook, yo, insert hook in same st or sp, pull up lp, yo, draw through 2 lps on hook (3 lps on hook), yo and draw through all 3 lps.

3-Bobble Stitch (3-bob): Yo, insert hook into st or sp indicated, pull up lp, yo, draw through 2 lps on hook, [yo, insert hook in same st or sp, pull up lp, yo, draw through 2 lps on hook] 2 times more (4 lps on hook), yo and draw through all 4 lps.

3-Treble Bobble (3tr-bob): Wrap yarn twice around hook, insert hook into st or sp indicated, pull up lp (4 lps on hook), [yo, draw through 2 lps on hook] 2 times (2 lps on hook), *wrap yarn twice around hook, insert hook in same st or sp, pull up lp, [yo, draw through 2 lps on hook] 2 times, rep from * once more (4 lps on hook), yo and draw through all 4 lps.

Note: The first Bobble Stitch in a round is started differently to subsequent bobbles in round. Instructions for the first bobble are included within the pattern. For subsequent bobbles follow the instructions above.

PATTERN

Base Round: Using Color A, ch 4; join with sl st to first ch to form a ring.

ROUND 1: (Right Side) Ch 3 (counts as first dc, now and throughout), 11 dc in ring; join with sl st to first dc (3rd ch of beg ch-3). (12 dc)

ROUND 2: Ch 1 (NOT counted as first st), sc in same st as joining, ch 5, skip next dc, [sc in next dc, ch 5, skip next dc] around; join with sl st to first sc. (6 sc & 6 ch-5 lps) Fasten off Color A and weave in all ends.

ROUND 3: With right side facing, join Color B with sl st to any ch-5 lp, ch 3, [yo, insert hook in same ch-5 lp, pull up lp, yo, draw through 2 lps on hook] 2 times (3 lps on hook), yo and draw through all 3 lps (first 3-bob made), ch 5, 3-bob in next ch-5 lp, ch 7, *3-bob in next lp, ch-5, 3 bob in next lp, ch 7; rep from * around; join with sl st to first dc (3rd ch of beg ch-3). (6 bobbles, 3 ch-5 lps & 3 ch-7 lps) Fasten off Color B and weave in all ends.

ROUND 4: With right side facing, join Color C with sl st to any ch-7 lp, ch 3, [yo, insert hook in same ch-7 lp, pull up lp, yo, draw through 2 lps on hook] 2 times (3 lps on hook), yo and draw through all 3 lps (first 3-bob made), ch 4, (3tr-bob, ch 4, 3-bob) in same lp, ch 5, sc in next ch-5 lp, ch 5, *(3-bob, ch 4, 3tr-bob, ch 4, 3-bob) in next ch-7 lp, ch 5, sc in next ch-5 lp, ch 5; rep from * around; join with sl st to first dc (3rd ch of beg ch-3) (9 bobbles, 3 sc, 6 ch-4 lps & 6 ch-5 lps) Fasten off Color C and weave in all ends.

ROUND 5: With right side facing, join Color D with sl st to first ch-4 lp (before tr-bob), ch 3, yo, insert hook in same lp, pull up lp, yo, draw through 2 lps on hook (3 lps on hook), yo, and draw through all 3 lps (first 2-bob made), ch 5, *2-bob in next lp, ch 5; rep from * around; join with sl st to first dc (3rd ch of beg ch-3) (12 bobbles & 12 ch-5 lps) Fasten off Color D and weave in all ends.

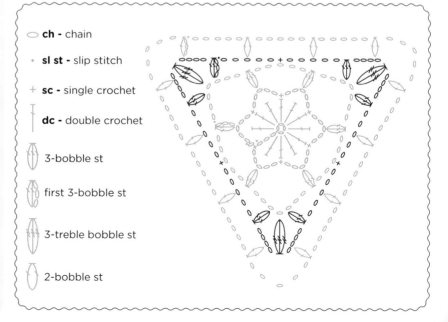

- ⬯ **ch -** chain
- • **sl st -** slip stitch
- + **sc -** single crochet
- | **dc -** double crochet
- **3-bobble st**
- **first 3-bobble st**
- **3-treble bobble st**
- **2-bobble st**

PATTERN

Base Round: Using Color A, ch 4; join with sl st to first ch to form a ring.

ROUND 1: (Right Side) Ch 6 (counts as first dc & ch-3), dc in ring, ch 5, *dc in ring, ch 3, dc in ring, ch 5; rep from * once more; join with sl st to first dc (3rd ch of beg ch-6). (6 dc, 3 ch-3 sps & 3 ch-5 lps) Fasten off Color A and weave in all ends.

ROUND 2: With right side facing, join Color B with sl st to any ch-5 lp, ch 3 (counts as first dc, now and throughout), (2 dc, ch 5, 3 dc) in same lp, ch 1, 3-bob in next ch-3 sp, ch 1, *(3 dc, ch 5, 3 dc) in next ch-5 lp, ch 1, 3-bob in next ch-3 sp, ch 1; rep from * around; join with sl st to first dc (3rd ch of beg ch-3). (18 dc, 3 bobbles, 6 ch-1 sps & 3 ch-5 lps) Fasten off Color B and weave in all ends.

ROUND 3: With right side facing, join Color C with sl st to any ch-5 lp, ch 3, (2 dc, ch 5, 3 dc) in same lp, [ch 2, 3-bob in next ch-1 sp] 2 times, ch 2, *(3 dc, ch 5, 3 dc) in next ch-5 lp, [ch 2, 3-bob in next ch-1 sp] 2 times, ch 2; rep from * around; join with sl st to first dc (3rd ch of beg ch-3). (18 dc, 6 bobbles, 18 ch-2 sps & 3 ch-5 lps) Fasten off Color C and weave in all ends

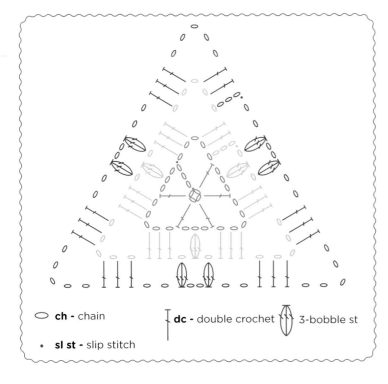

○ **ch -** chain

• **sl st -** slip stitch

| **dc -** double crochet   〈|〉 3-bobble st

Materials

Hook: E-4 (3.50 mm)

DMC Natura Just Cotton:
Color A – N 75 Moss Green
Color B – N 76 Bamboo
Color C – N 85 Giroflée

Finished Size: 4¼" (11 cm)

3-Bobble Stitch (3-bob): Yo, insert hook into st or sp indicated, pull up lp, yo, draw through 2 lps on hook, [yo, insert hook in same st or sp, pull up lp, yo, draw through 2 lps on hook] 2 times more (4 lps on hook), yo and draw through all 4 lps.

Motif 47

PATTERN

Base Round: Using Color A, ch 4; join with sl st to first ch to form a ring.

ROUND 1: (Right Side) Ch 3 (counts as first dc, now and throughout), 15 dc in ring; join with sl st to first dc (3rd ch of beg ch-3). (16 dc)

ROUND 2: Ch 3, dc in same st as joining, [2 dc in next dc] around; join with sl st to first dc (3rd ch of beg ch-3). (32 dc)

ROUND 3: Ch 1 (NOT counted as first st), sc in same st as joining, ch 11, sc in next dc, *sc in next dc, ch 11, sc in next dc; rep from * around; join with sl st to first sc. (32 sc & 16 ch-11 lps) Fasten off Color A and weave in all ends.

ROUND 4: With right side facing, join Color B with sl st to any ch-11 lp, ch 3, (2 dc, ch 3, 3 dc) in same lp, [(2 dc, ch 3, 3 dc) in next lp] around; join with sl st to first dc (3rd ch of beg ch-3). (16 shells) Fasten off and weave in all ends.

Materials
Hook: E-4 (3.50 mm)

DMC Natura Just Cotton:
Color A – N 06 Rose Layette
Color B – N 03 Sable

Finished Size: 5½" (14 cm)

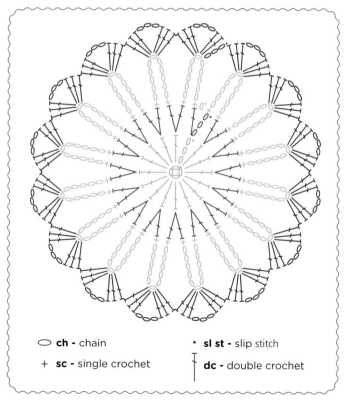

○ **ch** - chain   • **sl st** - slip stitch

+ **sc** - single crochet   ⊤ **dc** - double crochet

Motif 48

PATTERN

Base Round: Using Color A, ch 4; join with sl st to first ch to form a ring.

ROUND 1: (Right Side) Ch 5 (counts as first dc & ch-2), [dc in ring, ch 2] 11 times; join with sl st to first dc (3rd ch of beg ch-5). (12 dc & 12 ch-2 sps)

ROUND 2: Sl st in next ch-2 sp, ch 4 (counts as first tr), *wrap yarn twice around hook, insert hook in same sp, pull up lp, [yo, draw through 2 lps on hook] 2 times, rep from * once more (3 lps on hook), yo and draw through all 3 lps (first 3tr-bob made), [ch 5, 3tr-bob in next ch-2 sp] 11 times, ch 2; join with dc to first tr (4th ch of beg ch-4). This makes the last ch-5 lp and positions yarn for next round. (12 bobbles & 12 ch-5 lps)

ROUND 3: Ch 3 (counts as first dc), yo, insert hook in ch-5 lp under joining, pull up lp, yo, draw through 2 lps on hook (3 lps on hook), yo and draw through all 3 lps (first 2-bob made), ch 3, 2-bob in same lp, ch 5, *(2-bob, ch 3, 2-bob) in next ch-5 lp, ch 5; rep from * around; join with sl st to first dc (3rd ch of beg ch-3). (24 bobbles, 12 ch-3 sps & 12 ch-5 lps) Fasten off and weave in all ends.

Materials

Hook: E-4 (3.50 mm)

DMC Natura Just Cotton:
Color A – N 03 Sable

Finished Size: 4¾" (12 cm)

2-Bobble Stitch (2-bob): Yo, insert hook into st or sp indicated, pull up lp, yo, draw through 2 lps on hook, yo, insert hook in same st or sp, pull up lp, yo, draw through 2 lps on hook (3 lps on hook), yo and draw through all 3 lps.

3-Treble Bobble (3tr-bob): Wrap yarn twice around hook, insert hook into st or sp indicated, pull up lp (4 lps on hook), [yo, draw through 2 lps on hook] 2 times (2 lps on hook), *wrap yarn twice around hook, insert hook in same st or sp, pull up lp, [yo, draw through 2 lps on hook] 2 times, rep from * once more (4 lps on hook), yo and draw through all 4 lps.

Note: The first Bobble Stitch in a round is started differently to subsequent bobbles in round. Instructions for the first bobble are included within the pattern. For subsequent bobbles follow the instructions above.

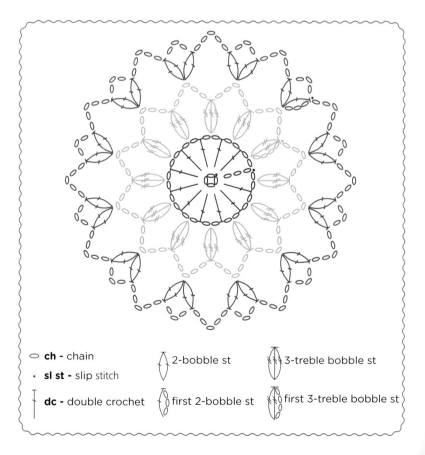

⌒ **ch** - chain

· **sl st** - slip stitch

┃ **dc** - double crochet

⟨⟩ 2-bobble st

⟨⟩ first 2-bobble st

⫰ 3-treble bobble st

⫰ first 3-treble bobble st

PATTERN

Base Round: Using Color A, ch 4; join with sl st to first ch to form a ring.

ROUND 1: (Right Side) Ch 4 (counts as first dc & ch-1, now and throughout), [dc in ring, ch 1] 11 times; join with sl st to first dc (3rd ch of beg ch-4). (12 dc & 12 ch-1 sps)

ROUND 2: Ch 3 (counts as first dc), yo, insert hook in same st as joining, pull up lp, yo, draw through 2 lps on hook (2 lps on hook), yo and draw through all lps (first 2-bob made), ch 7, [2-bob in next dc, ch 5] 2 times, *2-bob in next dc, ch 7, [2-bob in next dc, ch 5] 2 times; rep from * around; join with sl st to first dc (3rd ch of beg ch-3). (12 bobbles, 8 ch-5 lps & 4 ch-7 sps)

ROUND 3: Sl st in next ch-7 sp, ch 4, (dc, [ch 1, dc] 5 times) in same lp, ch 5, [sc in next ch-5 lp, ch 5] 2 times, *(dc, [ch 1, dc] 6 times) in same lp, ch 5, [sc in next ch-5 lp, ch 5] 2 times; rep from * around; join with sl st to first dc (3rd ch of beg ch-4). (28 dc, 24 ch-1 sps, 8 sc & 12 ch-5 lps)

ROUND 4: Ch 4, dc in next dc, [ch 1, dc in next dc] 5 times, ch 5, skip next ch-5 lp, sc in next ch-5 lp, ch 5, skip next ch-5 lp, *dc in next dc, [ch 1, dc in next dc] 6 times, ch 5, skip next ch-5 lp, sc in next ch-5 lp, ch 5, skip next ch-5 lp; rep from * around; join with sl st to first dc (3rd ch of beg ch-4). (28 dc, 24 ch-1 sps, 4 sc & 8 ch-5 lps) Fasten off and weave in all ends.

Materials:
Hook: E-4 (3.50 mm)

DMC Natura Just Cotton:
Color A – N 44 Agatha

Finished Size: 4¾″ (12 cm)

2-Bobble Stitch (2-bob): Yo, insert hook into st or sp indicated, pull up lp, yo, draw through 2 lps on hook, yo, insert hook in same st or sp, pull up lp, yo, draw through 2 lps on hook (3 lps on hook), yo and draw through all 3 lps.

Note: The first Bobble Stitch in a round is started differently to subsequent bobbles in round. Instructions for the first bobble are included within the pattern. For subsequent bobbles follow the instructions above.

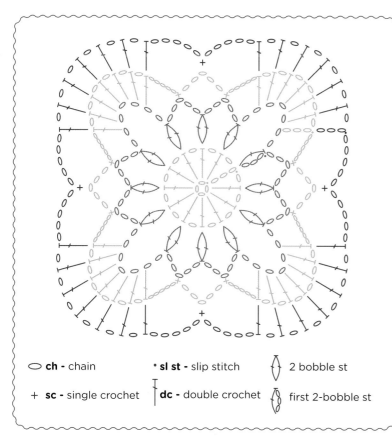

⬭ **ch -** chain	• **sl st -** slip stitch ⬧ 2 bobble st
+ **sc -** single crochet	**dc -** double crochet ⬧ first 2-bobble st

Motif 50

Materials
Hook: E-4 (3.50 mm)

DMC Natura Just Cotton:
Color A – N 03 Sable
Color B – N 05 Bleu Layette
Color C – N 06 Rose Layette

Finished Size: 4" (10 cm)

2-Bobble Stitch (2-bob): Yo, insert hook into st or sp indicated, pull up lp, yo, draw through 2 lps on hook, yo, insert hook in same st or sp, pull up lp, yo, draw through 2 lps on hook (3 lps on hook), yo and draw through all 3 lps.

3-Bobble Stitch (3-bob): Yo, insert hook into st or sp indicated, pull up lp, yo, draw through 2 lps on hook, [yo, insert hook in same st or sp, pull up lp, yo, draw through 2 lps on hook] 2 times more (4 lps on hook), yo and draw through all 4 lps.

Note: The first Bobble Stitch in a round is started differently to subsequent bobbles in round. Instructions for the first bobble are included within the pattern. For subsequent bobbles follow the instructions above.

PATTERN

Base Round: Using Color A, ch 4; join with sl st to first ch to form a ring.

ROUND 1: (Right Side) Ch 3 (counts as first dc, now and throughout), 2 dc in ring, ch 3, 3 dc in ring, ch 3] 3 times; join with sl st to first dc (3rd ch of beg ch-3). (12 dc & 4 ch-3 sps) Fasten off Color A and weave in all ends.

ROUND 2: With right side facing, join Color B with sl st to any ch-3 sp, ch 3, (3 dc, ch 3, 4 dc) in same sp, ch 1, *(4 dc, ch 3, 4 dc) in next ch-3 sp, ch 1; rep from * around; join with sl st to first dc (3rd ch of beg ch-3). (24 dc, 4 ch-1 sps & 4 ch-3 sps) Fasten off Color B and weave in all ends.

ROUND 3: With right side facing, join Color A with sl st to any ch-3 sp, ch 3, yo, insert hook in sp, pull up lp, yo, draw through 2 lps on hook (2 lps on hook), yo and draw through all lps (first 2-bob made), [ch 3, 2-bob] 2 times in same sp, ch 5, sc in next ch-1 sp, ch 5, *(2-bob, [ch 3, 2-bob] 2 times) in next ch-3 sp, ch 5, sc in next ch-1 sp, ch 5; rep from * around; join with sl st to first dc (3rd ch of beg ch-3). (12 bobbles, 8 ch-3 sps, 4 sc & 8 ch-5 lps) Fasten off Color A and weave in all ends.

ROUND 4: With right side facing, join Color C with sl st to first ch-3 sp, ch 3, [yo, insert hook in same sp, pull up lp, yo, draw through 2 lps on hook] 2 times (3 lps on hook), yo and draw through all 3 lps (first 3-bob made), ch 3, 3-bob in next ch-3 sp, ch 5, [sc in next ch-5 lp, ch 5] 2 times, *3-bob in next ch-3 sp, ch 3, 3-bob in next ch-3 sp, ch 5, [sc in next ch-5 lp, ch 5] 2 times; rep from * around; join with sl st to first dc (3rd ch of beg ch-3). (8 bobbles, 4 ch-3 sps, 8 sc & 12 ch-5 lps).

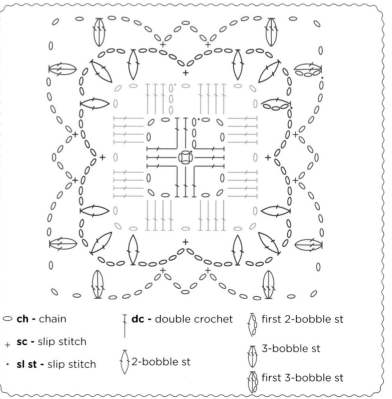

○ **ch** - chain
+ **sc** - slip stitch
· **sl st** - slip stitch

Ｉ **dc** - double crochet
◇ 2-bobble st

first 2-bobble st
3-bobble st
first 3-bobble st

PATTERN

Base Round: Using Color A, ch 4; join with sl st to first ch to form a ring.

ROUND 1: (Right Side) Ch 1 (NOT counted as first st), 6 sc in ring; join with sl st to first sc. (6 sc)

ROUND 2: Ch 4, (2tr-bob, ch 4, sl st) in same st as joining, *(sl st, ch 4, 2tr-bob, ch 4, sl st) in next sc; rep from * around; join with sl st to base of ch-4. (6 petals)

ROUND 3: Ch 8 (counts as first dc & ch-5), skip next petal, *dc between petals, ch 5, skip next petal; rep from * around; join with sl st to first dc (3rd ch of beg ch-8). (6 dc & 6 ch-5 lps)

ROUND 4: Ch 1, sc in same st as joining, (3 dc, ch 3, 3 dc) in next ch-5 lp, *sc in next dc, (3 dc, ch 3, 3 dc) in next ch-5 lp; rep from * around; join with sl st to first sc. (6 shells & 6 sc)

ROUND 5: Ch 6 (counts as first dc & ch-3), (2-bob, ch 3, 2-bob) in next ch-3 sp, ch 3, *dc in next sc, ch 3, (2-bob, ch 3, 2-bob) in next ch-3 sp, ch 3; rep from * around; join with sl st to first dc (3rd ch of beg ch-3). (12 bobbles, 6 dc & 18 ch-3 sps) Fasten off and weave in all ends.

Materials
Hook: E-4 (3.50 mm)

DMC Natura Just Cotton:
Color A – N 05 Bleu Layette

Finished Size: 4″ (10 cm)

2-Bobble Stitch (2-bob): Yo, insert hook into st or sp indicated, pull up lp, yo, draw through 2 lps on hook, yo, insert hook in same st or sp, pull up lp, yo, draw through 2 lps on hook (3 lps on hook), yo and draw through all 3 lps.

2-Treble Bobble (2tr-bob): Wrap yarn twice around hook, insert hook into st or sp indicated, pull up lp (4 lps on hook), [yo, draw through 2 lps on hook] 2 times (2 lps on hook), wrap yarn twice around hook, insert hook in same st or sp, pull up lp, [yo, draw through 2 lps on hook] 2 times (3 lps on hook), yo and draw through all 3 lps.

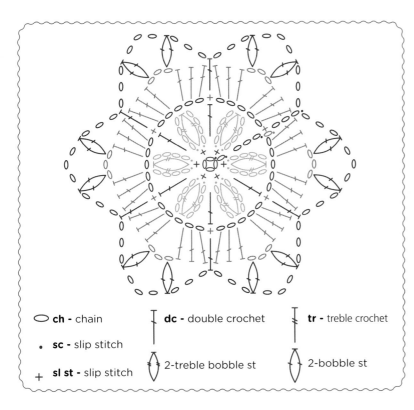

⬭ **ch -** chain

• **sc -** slip stitch

+ **sl st -** slip stitch

❘ **dc -** double crochet

⬮ 2-treble bobble st

❘ **tr -** treble crochet

⬮ 2-bobble st

Motif 52

PATTERN

Base Round: Using Color A, ch 4; join with sl st to first ch to form a ring.

ROUND 1: (Right Side) Ch 3 (counts as first dc, now and throughout), 2 dc in ring, ch 3, [3 dc in ring, ch 3] 3 times; join with sl st to first dc (3rd ch of beg ch-3). (12 dc & 4 ch-3 sps)

ROUND 2: Sl st in each of next 2 dc, sl st in next ch-3 sp, ch 3, (2 dc, ch 5, 3 dc) in same sp, ch 1, *(3 dc, ch 5, 3 dc) in next ch-3 sp, ch 1; rep from * around; join with sl st to first dc (3rd ch of beg ch-3). (24 dc, 4 ch-1 sps & 4 ch-5 lps)

ROUND 3: Ch 3, [yo, insert hook in next dc, pull up lp, yo, draw through 2 lps on hook] 2 times (3 lps on hook), yo and draw through all 3 lps (first cluster made), ch 1, (2-bob, ch 1, dc, ch 3, dc, ch 1, 2-bob) in next ch-5 lp, ch 1, *[3dc-cl (using next 3 dc), ch 1] 2 times, (2-bob, ch 1, dc, ch 3, dc, ch 1, 2-bob) in next ch-5 lp, ch 1; rep from * 2 times more, 3dc-cl (using next 3 dc), ch 1; join with sl st to first dc (3rd ch of beg ch-3). (8 bobbles, 8 clusters, 8 dc, 20 ch-1 sps & 4 ch-3 sps) Fasten off and weave in all ends.

Materials
Hook: E-4 (3.50 mm)

DMC Natura Just Cotton:
Color A – N 44 Agatha

Finished Size: 3¼" (8 cm)

2-Bobble Stitch (2-bob): Yo, insert hook into st or sp indicated, pull up lp, yo, draw through 2 lps on hook, yo, insert hook in same st or sp, pull up lp, yo, draw through 2 lps on hook (3 lps on hook), yo and draw through all 3 lps.

3-Double Crochet Cluster (3dc-cl): Yo, insert hook into st or sp indicated, pull up lp (3 lps on hook), yo, draw through 2 lps on hook (2 lps on hook), *yo, insert hook in next st or sp, pull up lp, yo, draw through 2 lps on hook; rep from * once more (4 lps on hook), yo and draw through all 4 lps.

Note: The first Bobble or Cluster Stitch in a round is started differently to subsequent bobbles in round. Instructions for the first bobble are included within the pattern. For subsequent bobbles follow the directions above.

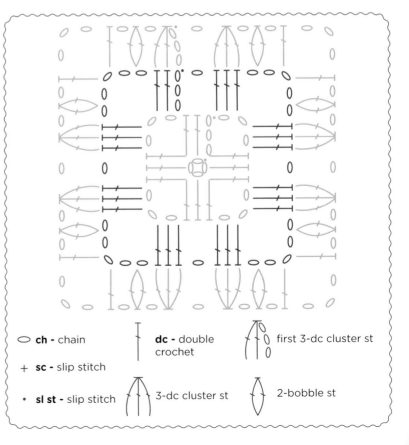

○ **ch** - chain

╎ **dc** - double crochet

first 3-dc cluster st

+ **sc** - slip stitch

• **sl st** - slip stitch

3-dc cluster st

2-bobble st

PATTERN

Base Round: Using Color A, ch 4; join with sl st to first ch to form a ring.

ROUND 1: (Right Side) Ch 1 (NOT counted as first st, now and throughout), 8 sc in ring; join with sl st to first sc. (8 sc)

ROUND 2: Ch 4 (counts as first tr), *wrap yarn twice around hook, insert hook in same st as joining, pull up lp, [yo, draw through 2 lps on hook] 2 times, rep from * once more (3 lps on hook), yo and draw through all 3 lps (first 3tr-bob made), ch 5, [3tr-bob in next sc, ch 5] around; join with sl st to first tr (4th ch of beg ch-4). (8 bobbles & 8 ch-5 lps) Fasten off Color A and weave in all ends.

ROUND 3: With right side facing, join Color B with sl st to any ch-5 lp, ch 1, sc in same lp, ch 5, [sc in next ch-5 lp, ch 5] around; join with sl st to first sc. (8 sc & 8 ch-5 lps)

ROUND 4: Sl st in next ch-5 lp, ch 3 (counts as first dc, (2 dc, ch 1, 3 dc) in same lp, ch 1, *(3 dc, ch 1, 3 dc) in same lp, ch 1; rep from * around; join with sl st to first dc (3rd ch of beg ch-3). (48 dc & 16 ch-1 sps) Fasten off Color B and weave in all ends.

ROUND 5: With right side facing, join Color C with sl st in any ch-1 sp, ch 1, (sc, ch 3, sc) in same sp, sc in each of next 2 dc, skip next dc, *(sc, ch 3, sc) in next ch-1 sp, sc in each of next 2 dc, skip next dc; rep from * around; join with sl st to first sc. (64 sc & 16 ch-3 sps) Fasten off Color C and weave in all ends.

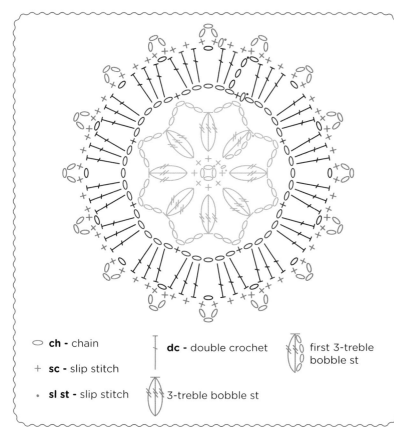

⬯ **ch** - chain		
+ **sc** - slip stitch		
sl st - slip stitch		

dc - double crochet

first 3-treble bobble st

3-treble bobble st

Materials
Hook: E-4 (3.50 mm)

DMC Natura Just Cotton:
Color A – N 83 Blé
Color B – N 79 Tilleul
Color C – N 76 Bamboo

Finished Size: 4″ (10 cm)

3-Treble Bobble (3tr-bob): Wrap yarn twice around hook, insert hook into st or sp indicated, pull up lp (4 lps on hook), [yo, draw through 2 lps on hook] 2 times (2 lps on hook), *wrap yarn twice around hook, insert hook in same st or sp, pull up lp, [yo, draw through 2 lps on hook] 2 times, rep from * once more (4 lps on hook), yo and draw through all 4 lps.

Note: The first Bobble Stitch in a round is started differently to subsequent bobbles in round. Instructions for the first bobble are included within the pattern. For subsequent bobbles follow the instructions above.

Motif 54

Materials
Hook: E-4 (3.50 mm)

DMC Natura Just Cotton:
Color A – N 02 Ivory
Color B – N 46 Forêt
Color C – N 05 Bleu Layette

Finished Size: 4″ (10 cm

2-Bobble Stitch (2-bob): Yo, insert hook into st or sp indicated, pull up lp, yo, draw through 2 lps on hook, yo, insert hook in same st or sp, pull up lp, yo, draw through 2 lps on hook (3 lps on hook), yo and draw through all 3 lps.

3-Bobble Stitch (3-bob): Yo, insert hook into st or sp indicated, pull up lp, yo, draw through 2 lps on hook, [yo, insert hook in same st or sp, pull up lp, yo, draw through 2 lps on hook] 2 times more (4 lps on hook), yo and draw through all 4 lps.

3-Double Crochet Cluster (3dc-cl): Yo, insert hook into st or sp indicated, pull up lp (3 lps on hook), yo, draw through 2 lps on hook (2 lps on hook), *yo, insert hook in next st or sp, pull up lp, yo, draw through 2 lps on hook; rep from * once more (4 lps on hook), yo and draw through all 4 lps.

Note: The first Bobble or Cluster Stitch in a round is started differently to subsequent bobbles in round. Instructions for the first bobble are included within the pattern. For subsequent bobbles follow the directions above.

PATTERN

Base Round: Using Color A, ch 4; join with sl st to first ch to form a ring.
ROUND 1: (Right Side) Ch 1 (NOT counted as first st, now and throughout), [sc in ring, ch 3] 4 times; join with sl st to first sc. (4 sc & 4 ch-3 sps) Fasten off Color A and weave in all ends.
ROUND 2: With right side facing, join Color B with sl st to any ch-3 sp, ch 3 (counts as first dc, now and throughout), (dc, ch 1, 2 dc) in same sp, ch 1, *(2 dc, ch 1, 2 dc) in same sp, ch 1; rep from * around; join with sl st to first dc (3rd ch of beg ch-3). (16 dc & 8 ch-1 sps)
ROUND 3: Ch 3, yo, insert hook in next dc, pull up lp, yo, draw through 2 lps on hook, yo, insert hook in next ch-1 sp, pull up lp, yo, draw through 2 lps on hook (3 lps on hook), yo and draw through all 3 lps (first cluster made), ch 5, *3dc-cl (using same ch-1 sp and next 2 dc), ch 3, dc in next ch-1 sp, ch 3, 3dc-cl (using next 2 dc & next ch-1 sp), ch 5; rep from * 2 times more, 3dc-cl (using same ch-1 sp and next 2 dc), ch 3, dc in next ch-1 sp, ch 3; join with sl st to first dc (3rd ch of beg ch-3). (8 clusters, 4 dc, 8 ch-3 sps, & 4 ch-5 lps) Fasten off Color B and weave in all ends.

ROUND 4: With right side facing, join Color C with sl st to any ch-5 lp, ch 3, (2 dc, ch 3, 3 dc) in same lp, ch 1, skip next cluster, (2-bob, ch 2, 2-bob) in next dc, ch 1, *(3 dc, ch 3, 3 dc) in next ch-5 lp, ch 1, skip next cluster, (2-bob, ch 2, 2-bob) in next dc, ch 1; rep from * around; join with sl st to first dc (3rd ch of beg ch-3). (8 bobbles, 24 dc, 4 ch-3 sps, 4 ch-2 sps & ch-1 sps) Fasten off Color C and weave in all ends.
ROUND 5: With right side facing, join Color B with sl st to any ch-3 sp, ch 3, [yo, insert hook in same sp, pull up lp, yo, draw through 2 lps on hook] 2 times (3 lps on hook), yo and draw through all 3 lps (first 3-bob made), ch 3, 3-bob in same sp, ch 5, sc in next ch-1 sp, ch 3, sc in next ch-2 sp, ch 3, sc in next ch 1 sp, ch 5, *(3-bob, ch 3, 3-bob) in next ch-3 sp, ch 5, sc in next ch-1 sp, ch 3, sc in next ch-2 sp, ch 3, sc in next ch 1 sp, ch 5; rep from * around; join with sl st to first dc (3rd ch of beg ch-3). (8 bobbles, 8 sc, 12 ch-3 sps & 8 ch-5 lps) Fasten off and weave in all ends.

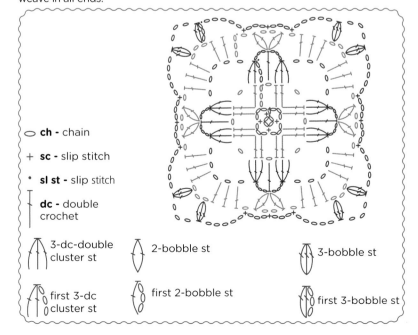

⬭ **ch** - chain

+ **sc** - slip stitch

• **sl st** - slip stitch

† **dc** - double crochet

⋀ **3-dc-double cluster st**

⬮ **2-bobble st**

⬮ **3-bobble st**

⋀ **first 3-dc cluster st**

⬮ **first 2-bobble st**

⬮ **first 3-bobble st**

PATTERN

Base Round: Using Color A, ch 4; join with sl st to first ch to form a ring.

ROUND 1: (Right Side) Ch 1 (NOT counted as first st, now and throughout), 12 sc in ring; join with sl st to first sc. (12 sc)

ROUND 2: Ch 1, sc in same st as joining, ch 5, skip next sc, *sc in next sc, ch 5, skip next sc; rep from * around; join with sl st to first sc. (6 sc & 6 ch-5 lps) Fasten off Color A and weave in all ends.

ROUND 3: With right side facing, join Color B with sl st to any ch-5 lp, ch 1, (sc, hdc, 3 dc, hdc, sc) in same lp, *(sc, hdc, 3 dc, hdc, sc) in next ch-5 lp; rep from * around; join with sl st to first sc. (6 petals)

ROUND 4: Ch 1, sc in sp between petals, ch 7, skip next petal, *sc in next sp between petals, ch 7, skip next petal; rep from * around; join with sl st to first sc. (6 sc & 6 ch-7 lps) Fasten off Color B and weave in all ends.

ROUND 5: With right side facing, join Color C with sl st to any ch-7 sp, ch 1, (sc, hdc, 5 dc, hdc, sc) in same lp, *(sc, hdc, 5 dc, hdc, sc) in next lp; rep from * around; join with sl st to first sc. (6 petals) Fasten off Color C and weave in all ends.

ROUND 6: With right side facing, join Color D with sl st to sp between petals, ch 4 (counts as first dc & ch 1), dc in same sp, ch 3, sc in 3rd (center) dc of 5-dc group, ch 3, *(dc, ch 1, dc) in next sp between petals, ch 3, sc in next center dc, ch 3; rep from * around; join with sl st to first dc (3rd ch of beg ch-4). (12 dc, 6 ch-1 sp, 6 sc & 12 ch-3 sps)

ROUND 7: Sl st in first ch-1 sp, ch 3 (counts as first dc),), [yo, insert hook in same sp, pull up lp, yo, draw through 2 lps on hook] 2 times (3 lps on hook), yo and draw through all 3 lps (first 3-bob made), ch 3, 3-bob in same sp, 3 dc in each of next 2 ch-3 sps, *(3-bob, ch 3, 3-bob) in next ch-1 sp, 3 dc in each of next 2 ch-3 sps; rep from * around; join with sl st to first dc (3rd ch of beg ch-3). (12 bobbles, 36 dc & 12 ch-3 sps) Fasten off Color D and weave in all ends.

Materials
Hook: E-4 (3.50 mm)

DMC Natura Just Cotton:
Color A – N 75 Moss Green
Color B – N 83 Blé
Color C – N 76 Bamboo
Color D – N 47 Safran

Finished Size: 4¼" (11 cm)

3-Bobble Stitch (3-bob): Yo, insert hook into st or sp indicated, pull up lp, yo, draw through 2 lps on hook, [yo, insert hook in same st or sp, pull up lp, yo, draw through 2 lps on hook] 2 times more (4 lps on hook), yo and draw through all 4 lps.

Note: The first Bobble Stitch in a round is started differently to subsequent bobbles in round. Instructions for the first bobble are included within the pattern. For subsequent bobbles follow the directions above.

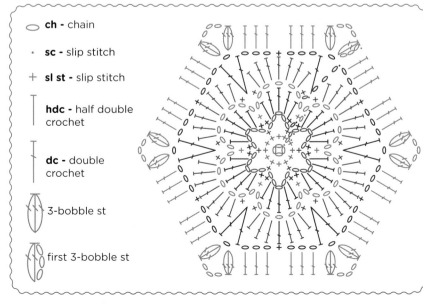

◯ **ch -** chain

· **sc -** slip stitch

+ **sl st -** slip stitch

| **hdc -** half double crochet

| **dc -** double crochet

3-bobble st

first 3-bobble st

Motif 56

Base Round: Using Color A, ch 4; join with sl st to first ch to form a ring.
ROUND 1: (Right Side) Ch 4 (counts as first dc & ch-1), [dc in ring, ch 1] 7 times; join with sl st to first dc (3rd ch of beg ch-4). (8 dc & 8 ch-1 sps) Fasten off Color A and weave in all ends.
ROUND 2: With right side facing, join Color B with sl st to any ch-1 sp, ch 1 (NOT counted as first st, now and throughout), (sc, ch 3, sc) in same sp, [(sc, ch 3, sc) in next ch-1 sp] around; join with sl st to first sc. (16 sc & 8 ch-3 sps) Fasten off Color B and weave in all ends.
ROUND 3: With right side facing, join Color C with sl st to any ch-3 sp, ch 3 (counts as first dc), (dc, ch 3, 2 dc) in same sp, ch 2, dc in next ch-3 sp, ch 2, *(2 dc, ch 3, 2 dc) in next sp, ch 2, dc in next sp, ch 2; rep from * around; join with sl st to first dc (3rd ch of beg ch-3). (20 dc, 16 ch-2 sps & 4 ch-3 sps) Fasten off Color C and weave in all ends.

ROUND 4: With right side facing, join Color D with sl st to any ch-3 sp, ch 1, (sc, ch 3, sc) in same sp, 2 sc in next 2 dc, [(sc, ch 3, sc) in next ch-2 sp] 2 times, sc in next dc, *(sc, ch 3, sc) in next ch-3 sp, sc in next dc, [(sc, ch 3, sc) in next ch-2 sp] 2 times, sc in next dc; rep from * around; join with sl st to first sc. (32 sc & 12 ch-3 sps) Fasten off Color D and weave in all ends.

Materials
Hook: E-4 (3.50 mm)

DMC Natura Just Cotton:
Color A – N 35 Nacar
Color B – N 76 Bamboo
Color C – N 87 Glacier
Color D – N 38 Liguen

Finished Size: 3¼" (8 cm)

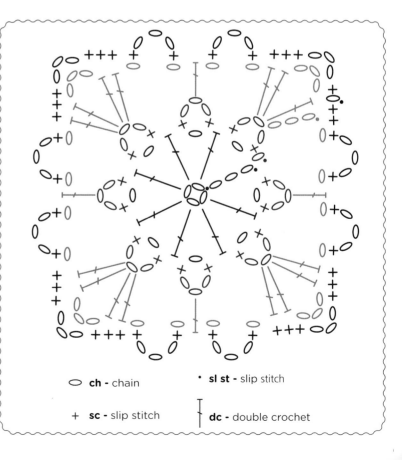

○ **ch** - chain   • **sl st** - slip stitch

+ **sc** - slip stitch   ⊤ **dc** - double crochet

PATTERN

Base Round: Using Color A, ch 4; join with sl st to first ch to form a ring.

ROUND 1: (Right Side) Ch 5 (counts as first dc & ch-2), [dc in ring, ch 2] 7 times; join with sl st to first dc (3rd ch of beg ch-5). (8 dc & 8 ch-2 sps) Fasten off Color A and weave in all ends.

ROUND 2: With right side facing, join Color B with sl st to any ch-2 sp, ch 3 (counts as first dc, now and throughout), yo, insert hook in same sp, pull up lp, yo, draw through 2 lps on hook (2 lps on hook), yo and draw through all lps (first 2-bob made), ch 1, 2-bob in same sp, ch 1, *(2-bob, ch1, 2-bob) in next sp, ch 1; rep from * around; join with sl st to first dc (3rd ch of beg ch-3). (16 bobbles & 16 ch-1 sps) Fasten off Color B and weave in all ends.

ROUND 3: With right side facing, join Color C with sl st to any ch-1 sp, ch 1 (NOT counted as first st, now and throughout), sc in same sp, ch 3, *sc in next sp, ch 3; rep from * around; join with sl st to first sc. (16 sc & 16 ch-3 sps) Fasten off Color C and weave in all ends.

ROUND 4: With right side facing, join Color D with sl st to any ch-3 sp, ch 3, 2 dc in same sp, ch 1, *3 dc in next sp, ch 1; rep from * around; join with sl st to first dc (3rd ch of beg ch-3). (48 dc & 16 ch-1 sps) Fasten off Color D and weave in all ends.

ROUND 5: With right side facing, join Color B with sl st to any ch-1 sp, ch 1, sc in same sp, ch 5, *sc in next sp, ch 5; rep from * around; join with sl st to first sc. (16 sc & 16 ch-5 lps) Fasten off Color B and weave in all ends.

ROUND 6: With right side facing, join Color E with sl st to any ch-5 lp, ch 1, (2 sc, ch 3, 2 sc) in same sp, *(2 sc, ch 3, 2 sc) in next ch-5 lp; rep from * around; join with sl st to first sc. (64 sc & 16 ch-3 sps) Fasten off Color E and weave in all ends.

Materials
Hook: E-4 (3.50 mm)

DMC Natura Just Cotton:
Color A – N 85 Giroflée
Color B – N 79 Tilleul
Color C – N 25 Aguamarin
Color D – N 47 Safran
Color E – N 31 Malva

Finished size: 4¾" (12 cm)

2-Bobble Stitch (2-bob): Yo, insert hook into st or sp indicated, pull up lp, yo, draw through 2 lps on hook, yo, insert hook in same st or sp, pull up lp, yo, draw through 2 lps on hook (3 lps on hook), yo and draw through all 3 lps.

Note: The first Bobble Stitch in a round is started differently to subsequent bobbles in round. Instructions for the first bobble are included within the pattern. For subsequent bobbles follow the directions above.

- **ch -** chain
- **sc -** slip stitch
- **sl st -** slip stitch
- **dc -** double crochet
- 2-bobble st
- first 2 bobble st

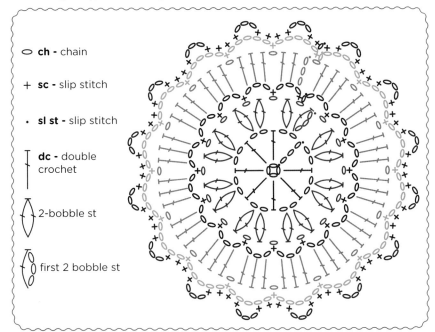

Motif 58

Materials
Hook: E-4 (3.50 mm)

DMC Natura Just Cotton:
Color A – N 79 Tilleul
Color B – N 83 Blé
Color C – N 44 Agatha
Color D – N 47 Safran
Color E – N 25 Aguamarina

Finished Size: 4¾" (12 cm)

Popcorn (PC): 4 dc in same st or sp indicated, drop lp from hook, insert hook from front to back in first dc made, pull dropped lp through.

Note: The first Popcorn Stitch in a round is started differently to subsequent bobbles in round. Instructions for the first bobble are included within the pattern. For subsequent bobbles follow the directions above.

PATTERN

Base Round: Using Color A, ch 4; join with sl st to first ch to form a ring.

ROUND 1: (Right Side) Ch 1 (NOT counted as first st, now and throughout), 8 sc in ring; join with sl st to first sc. (8 sc) Fasten off Color A and weave in all ends.

ROUND 2: With right side facing, join Color B with sl st to any sc, ch 3 (counts as first dc, now and throughout), 3 dc in same st, drop lp from hook, insert hook from front to back in first dc (3rd ch of beg ch-3), pull dropped lp through (first popcorn made), ch 2, *PC in next sc, ch 2; rep from * around; join with sl st to first dc (3rd ch of beg ch-3). (8 popcorns & 8 ch-2 sps) Fasten off Color B and weave in all ends.

ROUND 3: With right side facing, join Color C with sl st to any ch-2 sp, ch 3, 3 dc in same sp, ch 1, *4 dc in next ch-2 sp, ch 1; rep from * around; join with sl st to first dc (3rd ch of beg ch-3). (32 dc & 8 ch-1 sps) Fasten off Color C and weave in all ends.

ROUND 4: With right side facing, join Color D with sl st to any ch-1 sp, ch 1, sc in same sp, ch 5, *sc in next ch-1 sp, ch 5; rep from * around; join with sl st to first sc. (8 sc & 8 ch-5 lps) Fasten off Color D and weave in all ends.

ROUND 5: With right side facing, join Color C with sl st to any ch-5 lp, ch 3, 4 dc in same lp, ch 1, *5 dc in next lp, ch 1; rep from * around; join with sl st to first dc (3rd ch of beg ch-3). (40 dc & 8 ch-1 sps) Fasten off Color C and weave in all ends.

ROUND 6: With right side facing, join Color D with sl st to center dc of any 5-dc group, ch 1, sc in same st, ch 3, skip next 2 dc, sc in next ch-1 sp, ch 3, skip next 2 dc, *sc in next (center) dc, ch 3, skip next 2 dc, sc in next ch-1 sp, ch 3, skip next 2 dc; rep from * around; join with sl st to first sc. (16 sc & 16 ch-3 sps) Fasten off Color D and weave in all ends.

ROUND 7: With right side facing, join Color E with sl st to any ch-3 sp, ch 1, (2 sc, ch 3, 2 sc) in same sp, *(2 sc, ch 3, 2 sc) in next ch-3; rep from * around; join with sl st to first sc. (64 sc & 16 ch-3 sps) Fasten off and weave in all ends. Fasten off.

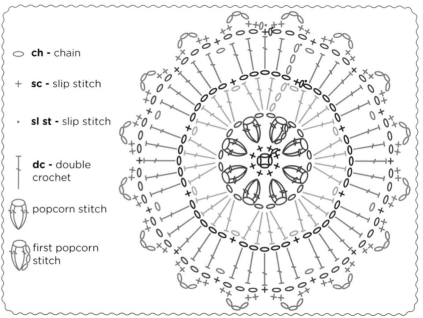

⌒ **ch -** chain

+ **sc -** slip stitch

• **sl st -** slip stitch

┃ **dc -** double crochet

popcorn stitch

first popcorn stitch

PATTERN

Base Round: Using Color A, ch 4; join with sl st to first ch to form a ring.

ROUND 1: (Right Side) Ch 1 (NOT counted as first st, now and throughout), 8 sc in ring; join with sl st to first sc. (8 sc) Fasten off Color A and weave in all ends.

ROUND 2: With right side facing, join Color B with sl st to any sc, ch 1, sc in same st, ch 4, 3tr-bob in next sc, ch 4, *sc in same sc, ch 4, 3tr-bob in next sc, ch 4; rep from * around; join with sl st to first sc. (4 bobbles, 4 sc & 8 ch-4 lps) Fasten off Color B and weave in all ends.

ROUND 3: With right side facing, join Color C with sl st to any sc, ch 8 (counts as first dc & ch-5, now and throughout), sc in next bobble, ch 5, *dc in next sc, ch 5, sc in next bobble, ch 5; rep from * around; join with sl st to first dc (3rd ch of beg ch-8). (4 dc, 4 sc & 8 ch-5 lps) Fasten off Color C and weave in all ends.

ROUND 4: With right side facing, join Color D with sl st to any sc, ch 8, dc in same sc, ch 3, sc in next ch-5 lp, ch 3, 3-bob in next dc, ch 3, sc in next ch-5 lp, ch 3, *(dc, ch 5, dc) in next sc, ch 3, sc in next ch-5 lp, ch 3, 3-bob in next dc, ch 3, sc in next ch-5 lp, ch 3; rep from * around; join with sl st to first dc (3rd ch of beg ch-8). (4 bobbles, 8 dc, 8 sc, 16 ch-3 sps & 4 ch-5 lps) Fasten off Color D and weave in all ends.

ROUND 5: With right side facing, join Color E with sl st to any ch-5 lp, ch 1, (2 sc, ch 5, 2 sc) in same lp, [(sc, ch 3, sc) in next ch-3 sp] 4 times, *(2 sc, ch 5, 2 sc) in next ch-5 lp, [(sc, ch 3, sc) in next ch-3 sp] 4 times; rep from * around; join with sl st to first sc. (48 sc, 16 ch-3 sps & 4 ch-5 lps) Fasten off Color E and weave in all ends.

Materials
Hook: E-4 (3.50 mm)

DMC Natura Just Cotton:
Color A – N 76 Bamboo
Color B – N 05 Bleu Layette
Color C – N 31 Malva
Color D – N 49 Turquoise
Color E – N 06 Rose Layette

Finished Size: 4" (10 cm)

3-Bobble Stitch (3-bob): Yo, insert hook into st or sp indicated, pull up lp, yo, draw through 2 lps on hook, [yo, insert hook in same st or sp, pull up lp, yo, draw through 2 lps on hook] 2 times more (4 lps on hook), yo and draw through all 4 lps.

3-Treble Bobble (3tr-bob): Wrap yarn twice around hook, insert hook into st or sp indicated, pull up lp (4 lps on hook), [yo, draw through 2 lps on hook] 2 times (2 lps on hook), *wrap yarn twice around hook, insert hook in same st or sp, pull up lp, [yo, draw through 2 lps on hook] 2 times, rep from * once more (4 lps on hook), yo and draw through all 4 lps.

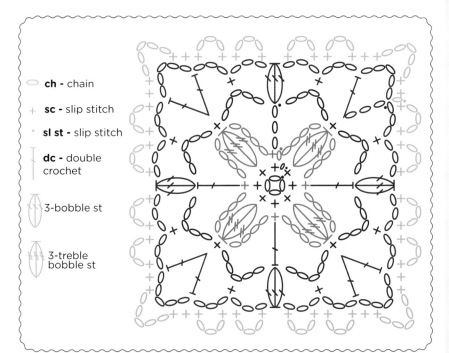

⬭ **ch -** chain

＋ **sc -** slip stitch

° **sl st -** slip stitch

dc - double crochet

3-bobble st

3-treble bobble st

Motif 60

PATTERN

Base Round: Using Color A, ch 4; join with sl st to first ch to form a ring.

ROUND 1: (Right Side) Ch 6 (counts as first dc & ch 3, now and throughout), [dc in ring, ch 3] 5 times; join with sl st to first dc (3rd ch of beg ch-6). (6 dc & 6 ch-3 sps)

ROUND 2: Sl st in first ch-3 sp, ch 3 (counts as first dc, now and throughout), 3 dc in same sp, ch 3, [4 dc in next ch-3 sp, ch 3] around; join with sl st to first dc (3rd ch of beg ch-3). (24 dc & 6 ch-3 sps)

ROUND 3: Ch 6, skip next dc-group, [(2 dc, ch 3, 2 dc) in next ch-3 sp, ch 3] 5 times, (2 dc, ch 3, dc) in last ch-3 sp; join with sl st to first dc (3rd ch of beg ch-6). (24 dc & 12 ch-3 sps)

ROUND 4: Sl st in first ch-3 sp, ch 3, 3 dc in same sp, ch 1, (2 dc, ch 3, 2 dc) in next ch-3 sp, ch 1, *4 dc in next ch-3 sp, ch 1, (2 dc, ch 3, 2 dc) in next ch-3 sp, ch 1; rep from * around; join with sl st to first dc (3rd ch of beg ch-3). (48 dc, 6 ch-3 sps & 12 ch-1 sps)

ROUND 5: Ch 1 (NOT counted as first st, now and throughout), sc in same st as joining, [sc in next st or sp] around, working 3 sc in each corner ch-3 sp; join with sl st to first sc. (78 sc) Fasten off and weave in all ends.

ROUND 6: With right side facing, join Color B with sl st to any sc, ch 1, sc in each sc around; join with sl st to first sc. (78 sc) Fasten off Color B and weave in all ends.

Materials
Hook: E-4 (3.50 mm)

DMC Natura Just Cotton:
Color A – N 25 Aguamarina
Color B – N 75 Moss Green

Finished Size: 4¾" (12 cm)

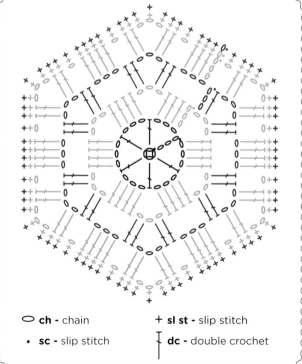

⬭ **ch** - chain   + **sl st** - slip stitch

• **sc** - slip stitch   ⊤ **dc** - double crochet

Projects

Summer Bag

Materials

Hook: H-8 (5.00 mm)

DMC Natura XL:
Colors:
Color A – N 73 Light Blue
        N 91 Light Yellow
Color B – N 82 Chartreuse
Color C – N 07 Sea Green

Bag handles
Fabric for lining

<u>**Finished Size:**</u> 15¾" x 15¾"
(40 x 40 cm)

This project uses Motif 1 on page 22

PATTERN

Following instructions for Motif 1, use the following color-ways to make a total of 18 motifs.

Block 1 – Make 9 Motifs
Color A – N 73 Light Blue
Color B – N 82 Chartreuse

Block 2 – Make 9 Motifs
Color A - N 91 Light Yellow
Color B – N 82 Chartreuse

Assembly of Bag
Use photo and layout diagram as guide.

With right sides facing, lay out 9 motifs in a 3 x 3 square (one Side of Bag), alternating Blocks 1 & 2. Repeat with remaining 9 motifs (other Side of Bag).

Layout For Both Sides of Bag

Motif Joining
For each side, work across horizontal seams first.

♥Holding first two motifs together, with right sides facing (wrong sides together), working through both thicknesses, matching sts, working in back loops only, using Color C, join with sl st to corresponding center chs of corner ch-3 groups, ch 1, sc in same ch, *sc in each st or ch across to center ch of next corner**, pick up next two motifs and starting from center ch of new corner, rep from * across seam, ending at ** on final repeat. Fasten off and weave in all ends.
Repeat from ♥ for the remaining horizontal seam.
Repeat from ♥ for both vertical seams.

Repeat the Motif Joining for the second side.

Bag Joining
Holding the finished two sides together, with right sides facing, using the same method established, starting from a corner, join around only 3 sides, working (sc, ch 1, sc) in each of the two corners. DO NOT FINISH OFF.

TOP EDGING

ROUND 1: With right side facing, ch 1 (NOT counted as first st, now and throughout), working through single thickness around top of Bag, sc in back loops of each st or ch around; join with sl st to first sc.
ROUND 2: Ch 1, working in both loops, sc in each sc around; join with sl st to first sc. Fasten off and weave in all ends.

Sew the fabric lining inside the bag and attach the handles.

Materials

Hook: E-4 (3.50 mm)

DMC Natura just Cotton:
Colors:
Color A – N 51 Erica
Color B – N 85 Giroflée
          N 75 Moss Green
Color C – N 74 Curry
Color D – N 05 Bleu Layette
Color E – N 64 Prussian

Ribbon or Cord for Waistband Tie

Finished Size: 16½" x 21"
(42 x 53 cm)

This project uses Motif 2 on page 24

PATTERN

Following instructions for Motif 2, use the following color-ways to make a total of 84 motifs.

Block 1 – Make 42 Motifs
Color A – N 51 Erica
Color B – N 85 Giroflée
Color C – N 74 Curry

Block 2 – Make 42 Motifs
Color A – N 51 Erica
Color B – N 75 Moss Green
Color C – N 74 Curry

Assembly of Skirt
Use photo and layout diagram as guide.

With right sides facing, using 42 motifs, lay out 6 motifs across by 7 motifs down (either Front or Back of Skirt), alternating Blocks 1 & 2. Repeat with remaining 42 motifs so that both Front and Back look the same.

Layout of both Front & Back of Skirt (Make 2)

Motif Joining
For Front and Back, work across horizontal seams first.
♥Holding first two motifs together, with right sides facing (wrong sides together), working through both thicknesses, matching sts, working in back loops only, using Color D, join with sl st to corresponding chs of corner ch-2 sps, ch 1, sc in same ch, *sc in each st or ch across to next corner ch**, pick up next two motifs and starting from corner ch of new motif, rep from * across seam, ending at ** on final repeat. Fasten off and weave in all ends.
Repeat from ♥ for the remaining horizontal seams.
Repeat from ♥ for all vertical seams.

Repeat the Motif Joining for the remaining Front/Back

Skirt Seams
Holding the finished Front and Back together, with right sides facing, using the same method established, starting from a corner, join across length of skirt (7 motifs). Fasten off and weave in all ends.
Repeat seam on the other side of Skirt.

WAISTBAND

ROUND 1: With right side facing, working around top of Skirt, join Color D with sl st to ch-2 sp, ch 1 (NOT counted as first st, now and throughout), 2 sc in same sp, [2 sc in next ch-2 sp] around; join with sl st to first sc. Fasten off Color D and weave in all ends.
ROUND 2: With right side facing, join Color C with sl st to any sc, ch 1, sc in same st, [sc in next sc] around; join with sl st to first sc.
ROUNDS 3-4: Ch 1, sc in each sc around; join with sl st to first sc.
ROUND 5: Ch 3 (counts as first dc), [dc in next dc] around; join with sl st to first dc (3rd ch of beg ch-3).
ROUNDS 6-7: Rep Rounds 3-4.

At the end of Round 7, fasten off Color C and weave in all ends.

Weave Ribbon or Cord through stitches in Round 5 and tie in front.

HEM EDGING

ROUND 1: With right side facing, working around bottom of Skirt, join Color C with sl st to any st or sp, ch 1 (NOT counted as first st, now and throughout), sc in same st, [sc in next st or sp] around; join with sl st to first sc.

ROUND 2: Ch 1, sc in each sc around; join with sl st to first sc. Fasten off Color C and weave in all ends.

ROUND 3: With right side facing, join Color E with sl st to any sc, ch 1, sc in same st, sc in each of next 2 sc, (sc, ch 3, sc) in next sc, *sc in each of next 3 sc, (sc, ch 3, sc) in next sc; rep from * around; join with sl st to first sc. Fasten off Color E and weave in all ends.

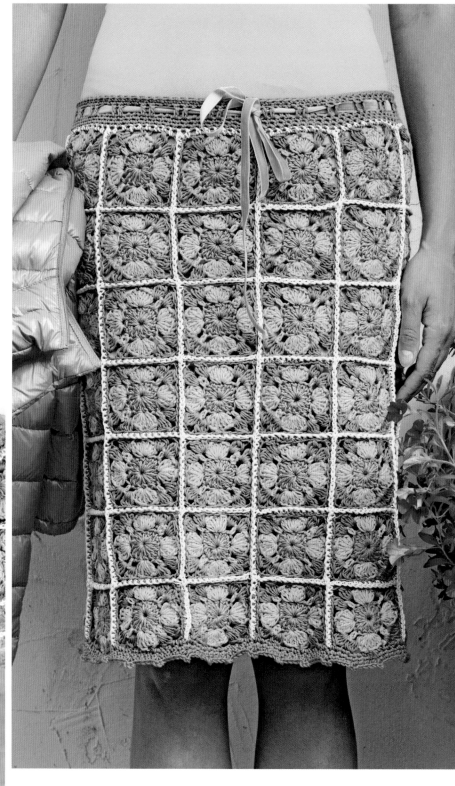

Materials

Hook: E-4 (3.50 mm)

DMC Natura Just Cotton:
Colors:
Color A – N 43 Golden Lemon
              N 03 Sable
Color B – N 26 Blue Jeans
Color C – N 49 Turquoise
Color D – N 43 Golden Lemon

<u>**Finished Size:**</u> 17½" (44 cm) circumference, length 12" (30 cm)

This project uses Motif 3 on page 26

PATTERN

Following instructions for Motif 3, use the following color-ways to make a total of 24 motifs.

Block 1 – Make 12 Motifs
Color A – N 43 Golden Lemon
Color B – N 26 Blue Jeans

Block 2 – Make 12 Motifs
Color A – N 03 Sable
Color B – N 26 Blue Jeans

Assembly of Hat
Use photo and layout diagram as guide.

With right sides facing, using all motifs, lay out 6 motifs across by 4 motifs down, alternating Blocks 1 & 2.

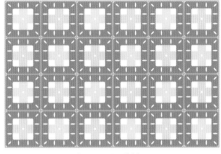

Layout of Hat

Motif Joining
Work across horizontal seams first. ♥Holding first two motifs together, with right sides facing (wrong sides together), working through both thicknesses, matching sts, working in back loops only, using Color C, join with sl st to corresponding chs of corner ch-1 sps, ch 1, sc in same ch, *sc in each st or ch across to next corner ch**, pick up next two motifs and starting from corner ch of new motif, rep from * across seam, ending at ** on final repeat. Fasten off and weave in all ends.

Repeat from ♥ for the remaining horizontal seams.
Repeat from ♥ for all vertical seams.

Hat Seam
Fold Hat in half, with right sides facing, using the same method above, starting from a corner, join across length of Hat (4 motifs) and across top of Hat. Fasten off and weave in all ends.

HAT BAND

ROUND 1: With right side facing, working around brim of Hat, join Color C with sl st to back loop of any st or sp, ch 1 (NOT counted as first st, now and throughout), sc in same st, [sc in next st or sp] around; join with sl st to first sc.

ROUNDS 2-3: Ch 1, sc in each sc around; join with sl st to first sc.
At the end of Round 3, fasten off Color C and weave in all ends.

ROUND 4: With right side facing, join Color D with sl st to any sc, ch 1, sc in same st, [sc in next sc] around; join with sl st to first sc. Fasten off Color D and weave in all ends.

ROUND 5: With right side facing, join Color B with sl st to any sc, ch 1, sc in same st, [sc in next sc] around; join with sl st to first sc. Fasten off Color B and weave in all ends.

ROUND 6: With right side facing, join Color C with sl st to any sc, ch 1, sc in same st, [sc in next sc] around; join with sl st to first sc.

ROUND 7: Ch 1, sc in each sc around; join with sl st to first sc. Fasten off Color C and weave in all ends.

Rug

Materials

Hook: J-10 (6.00 mm)

DMC Natura XL:
Colour:
Color A – N 03 Off-White
(10 balls)

Finished Size: 27½" x 39½"
(70 x 100 cm)

This project uses Motif 4 on page 28

PATTERN

Following instructions for Motif 4, make a total of 24 motifs.

Assembly of Rug
Use photo as guide.

With right sides facing, using all motifs, lay out 6 motifs across by 4 motifs down.

Motif Joining
Work across horizontal seams first. ♥Holding first two motifs together, with right sides facing (wrong sides together), working through both thicknesses, matching sts, working in back loops only, join with sl st to corresponding chs of corner ch-1 sps, ch 1, sc in same ch, *sc in each st or ch across to next corner ch**, pick up next two motifs and starting from corner ch of new motif, rep from * across seam, ending at ** on final repeat. Fasten off and weave in all ends.

Repeat from ♥ for the remaining horizontal seams.
Repeat from ♥ for all vertical seams.

At the end of the last seam, DO NOT FINISH OFF.

SHELL EDGING

ROUND 1: With right side facing, ch 3 (NOT counted as first st, now and throughout), dc in each dc or sp around; join with sl st to first sc.
ROUND 2: Ch 1, sc in same st as joining, skip next 2 dc, 6 dc in next dc, skip next 2 dc, *sc in next dc, skip next 2 dc, 6 dc in next dc, skip next 2 dc; rep from * around; join with sl st to first sc. Fasten off and weave in all ends.

Leg Warmers

Materials

Hook: E-4 (3.50 mm)

DMC Natura Just Cotton:
Colors:
Color A – N 06 Rose Layette
             N 80 Salomé
Color B – N 38 Liquen

Ribbon or Cord for Ties

<u>**Finished Size:**</u> 12½″ (32 cm) circumference and 17½″ (45 cm) length

This project uses Motif 5 on page 30

PATTERN

Following instructions for Motif 5, use the following color-ways to make a total of 48 motifs.

Block 1 – Make 24 Motifs
Color A – N 06 Rose Layette
Color B – N 38 Liquen

Block 2 – Make 24 Motifs
Color A – N 80 Salomé
Color B – N 38 Liquen

Assembly of Leg Warmers
Use photo and layout diagram as guide.

With right sides facing, using 24 motifs, lay out 4 motifs across by 6 motifs down (one Leg Warmer), alternating Blocks 1 & 2. Repeat with remaining 24 motifs so that both Leg Warmers look the same.

Motif Joining
Work across horizontal seams first. ♥Holding first two motifs together, with right sides facing (wrong sides together), working through both thicknesses, matching sts, working in back loops only, using Color B, join with sl st to corresponding chs of corner ch-1 sps, ch 1, sc in same ch, *sc in each st or ch across to next corner ch**, pick up next two motifs and starting from corner ch of new motif, rep from * across seam, ending at ** on final repeat. Fasten off and weave in all ends.

Repeat from ♥ for the remaining horizontal seams.
Repeat from ♥ for all vertical seams.

Repeat the Motif Joining for the second Leg Warmer.

Layout of Leg Warmer (Make 2)

Side Seam
Fold Leg Warmer in half, with right sides facing, using the same method above, starting from a corner, join across length (6 motifs) to form tube. DO NOT FINISH OFF.

TOP EDGING
ROUND 1: With right side facing, ch 1 (NOT counted as first st, now and throughout), sc in each st or sp around; join with sl st to first sc.
ROUND 2: Ch 1, sc in each sc around; join with sl st to first sc.
ROUND 3: Ch 3 (counts as first dc), [dc in next sc] around; join with sl st to first dc (3rd ch of beg ch-3).
ROUND 4: Rep Round 2.
ROUND 5: Ch 1, sc in same st as joining, sc in each of next 2 sc, (sc, ch 3, sc) in next sc, *sc in each of next 3 sc, (sc, ch 3, sc) in next sc; rep from * around; join with sl st to first sc. Fasten off Color B and weave in all ends.

Weave Ribbon or Cord through stitches in Round 3 and tie at outer sides.

BOTTOM EDGING
ROUND 1: With right side facing, join Color B with sl st to any st or sp on bottom edge, ch 1, sc in same st or sp, [sc in next st or sp] around; join with sl st to first sc.
ROUND 2: Ch 1, sc in same st as joining, sc in each of next 2 sc, (sc, ch 3, sc) in next sc, *sc in each of next 3 sc, (sc, ch 3, sc) in next sc; rep from * around; join with sl st to first sc. Fasten off Color B and weave in all ends.

Repeat Side Seam, Top & Bottom Edging, on second Leg Warmer.

Small Purse

Materials

Hook: E-4 (3.50 mm)

DMC Natura Just Cotton:
Colors
Color A – N 35 Nacar

Purse Frame
Yarn Needle (if needed)
Ribbon or Cord for Handle.

Finished Size: 6″ x 8½″ (15 cm x 22 cm)

This project uses Motif 6 on page 32

PATTERN

Following instructions for Motif 6, and the join-as-you-go method on Round 4 (instructions below) make a total of 22 motifs – 11 for each Side of the Purse. Using layout diagram as guide, join motifs together.

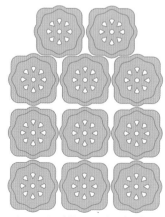

Layout of Purse (make 2).

SIDE OF PURSE (Make 2)

First Motif

ROUNDS 1-4: Repeat Rounds 1-4 of Motif 6.

Motifs 2-11

ROUNDS 1-3: Repeat Rounds 1-3 of Motif 6.

For One-Sided Join:
ROUND 4: (Joining Round) Sl st in first ch-5 lp, ch 1, (NOT counted as first st, now and throughout), (sc, hdc, dc) in same lp, working in previous motif, sl st in corresponding corner ch-1 sp, working in current motif, (dc, hdc, sc) in same lp, working in previous motif, sl st in next ch-1 sp, working on current motif, 3 sc in next ch-3 lp, working on previous motif, sl st in next ch-1 sp, working on current motif, (sc, hdc, dc) in next ch-5 lp, working on previous motif, sl st in next corner ch-1 sp (one side of motifs joined), (dc, hdc, sc) in same lp, ch 1, 3 sc in next ch-3 lp, ch 1, *(sc, hdc, dc, ch 1, dc, hdc, sc) in next ch-5 lp, ch 1, 3 sc in next ch-3 lp, ch 1; rep from * around; join with sl st to first sc. Fasten off and weave in all ends.

For Two-Sided Join:

ROUND 4: (Joining Round) Sl st in first ch-5 lp, ch 1, (sc, hdc, dc) in same lp, working in first previous motif, sl st in corresponding corner ch-1 sp, working in current motif, (dc, hdc, sc) in same lp, working in first previous motif, sl st in next ch-1 sp, working on current motif, 3 sc in next ch-3 lp, working on first previous motif, sl st in next ch-1 sp, working on current motif, (sc, hdc, dc) in next ch-5 lp, working on first previous motif, sl st in next corner ch-1 sp (one side of motifs joined), (dc, hdc, sc) in same lp, working in next previous motif, sl st in next ch-1 sp, working on current motif, 3 sc in next ch-3 lp, working on next previous motif, sl st in next ch-1 sp, working on current motif, (sc, hdc, dc) in next ch-5 lp, working on next previous motif, sl st in next corner ch-1 sp (two sides), (dc, hdc, sc) in same lp, ch 1, 3 sc in next ch-3 lp, ch 1, ch 1, 3 sc in next ch-3 lp, ch 1, (sc, hdc, dc, ch 1, dc, hdc, sc) in next ch-5 lp, ch 1, 3 sc in next ch-3 lp, ch 1; join with sl st to first sc. Fasten off and weave in all ends.

Repeat for other Side of Purse.

Purse Seam
Holding the two Sides together, with right sides facing (wrong sides together), working through both thicknesses along the length of the Sides, matching sts, join with sl st to corresponding center chs of corner ch-1 sps, ch 1, sc in same ch, [sc in next st or ch] across only 3 sides, working (sc, ch 1, sc) in both corner ch-1 sps. Fasten off and weave in all ends.

Attach top of Purse to Frame (using yarn needle if necessary).
Attach Ribbon or Cord to form Handle.

Shawl

Materials

Hook: E-4 (3.50 mm)

DMC Natura Just Cotton: Colors:
Color A – N 35 Nacar
Color B – N 09 Gris Argent

Finished Size: 20" x 43" (50 x 110 cm)

This project uses Motif 7 on page 34

PATTERN

Following instructions for Motif 7, and the join-as-you-go method on Round 3 (instructions below) make a total of 40 motifs using the following color-ways:

Block 1 – Make 29 Motifs
Color A – N 35 Nacar
Color B – N 09 Gris Argent

Block 2 – Make 11 Motifs
Color A – N 09 Gris Argent
Color B – N 35 Nacar

CENTER OF SHAWL

First Motif

ROUNDS 1-3: Repeat Rounds 1-3 of Motif 7.

Motifs 2-6

ROUNDS 1-2: Repeat Rounds 1-2 of Motif 7.
ROUND 3: (Joining Round) Ch 1, (NOT counted as first st, now and throughout), sc in sp between last and first hdc (sp directly under join), 4 hdc in next ch-2 sp, working in 7th petal of previous motif, sl st in 4th hdc, working in current motif, 4 hdc in same sp, sc in sp between next 2 hdc, 4 hdc in next ch-2 sp, working in 8th petal of previous motif, sl st in 4th hdc, working in current motif, 4 hdc in same sp (join complete),

*sc in sp between next 2 hdc, 8 hdc in next ch-2 sp; rep from * around; join with sl st to first sc. Fasten off Color B and weave in all ends.

These joined 6 Motifs form the center of the Shawl.

FIRST HALF OF SHAWL

Motifs 7-23

Using layout diagram as guide, repeat Motif 2, joining motifs as established, from Center strip outwards, to form one half of the Shawl.

SECOND HALF OF SHAWL

Motifs 24-40

Rotate the Shawl and using layout diagram as guide, repeat Motif 2, joining motifs as established, from Center strip outwards, to form complete Shawl.

Materials

Hook: E-4 (3.50 mm)

DMC Natura Just CottonColors:

Color A – N 49 Turquoise
      N 82 Lobelia
      N 43 Golden Lemon
      N 49 Turquoise
Color B – N 82 Lobelia
      N 83 Blé
      N 52 Geranium
      N 18 Coral
Color C – N 43 Golden Lemon
      N 52 Geranium
      N 82 Lobelia
      N 83 Blé
Color D – N 18 Coral
      N 82 Lobelia
Color E – N 83 Blé
      N 43 Golden Lemon
Color F – N 49 Turquoise

Finished Size: 14" (36 cm) wide & 44" (112 cm) circumference

This project uses Motif 8 on page 36

Popcorn (PC): 4 dc in same st or sp indicated, drop lp from hook, insert hook from front to back in first dc made, pull dropped lp through.

PATTERN

Following instructions for Motif 8, and the join-as-you-go method on Round 6 (instructions below) make a total of 16 motifs using the following color-ways. The layout is 8 motifs around and 2 motifs wide.

Block 1 – Make 4 Motifs
Color A – N 49 Turquoise
Color B – N 82 Lobelia
Color C – N 43 Golden Lemon
Color D – N 18 Coral
Color E – N 83 Blé

Block 2 – Make 4 Motifs
Color A – N 82 Lobelia
Color B – N 83 Blé
Color C – N 52 Geranium
Color D – N 18 Coral
Color E – N 43 Golden Lemon

Block 3 – Make 4 Motifs
Color A – N 43 Golden Lemon
Color B – N 52 Geranium
Color C – N 82 Lobelia
Color D – N 18 Coral
Color E – N 43 Golden Lemon

Block 4 – Make 4 Motifs
Color A – N 49 Turquoise
Color B – N 18 Coral
Color C – N 83 Blé
Color D – N 82 Lobelia
Color E – N 43 Golden Lemon

First Motif (Block 1)

ROUNDS 1-6: Repeat Rounds 1-6 of Motif 8.

Motifs 2-16
Use photo and layout diagram as guide for color-way, Block placement and joining sides.
Note: Remember to join the end motifs to form a circular strip.
ROUNDS 1-5: Repeat Rounds 1-5 of Motif 8.

ROUND 6: Rep Round 6 of Motif 8, working the following across the side(s) for joining (from one corner to next corner):

Joining Side: (Start as established until corner for joining, then:) Ch 1, working in previous motif, sl st in corresponding corner ch-3 sp, ch1, *working in current motif, 4 dc in next ch-5 lp, ch 2, working in previous motif, sl st in next ch-4 lp, ch 1; rep from * once more, 4 dc in next ch-5 lp, ch 1, working in previous motif, sl st in corresponding corner ch-3 sp, ch1, working in current motif, (continue with the next 4 dc, etc.).

BORDER

ROUND 1: With right side facing, join Color F with sl st to any sp between two motifs, ch 1 (NOT counted as first st, now and throughout), sc in same sp, [3 sc in next st or sp] around; join with sl st to first sc.
ROUND 2: Ch 1, sc in same st as joining, *ch 6, PC in 3rd ch from hook, ch 3, skip next 2 sc**, sc in next sc; rep from * around, ending at ** on final repeat; join with sl st to first sc. Fasten off and weave in all ends.

Repeat Border on other side of Cowl.

Market Bag

Materials

Hook: E-4 (3.50 mm)

DMC Natura Just Cotton:
Colors:
Color A – N 79 Tilleul
Color B – N 25 Aguamarina
      N 20 Jade
      N 54 Green Smoke
Color C – N 30 Glicine
Color D – N 20 Jade

2 x 36" (90 cm) Straps

Finished Size: 15¾" (40 cm) long
& 15¼" (39 cm) circumference)

This project uses Motif 9 on page 38

PATTERN

Following instructions for Motif 9, and the join-as-you-go method on Round 5 (instructions below) make a total of 26 motifs using the following color-ways. The layout is 8 motifs around and 3 motifs down, plus 2 motifs at base of Bag.

Block 1 – Make 10 Motifs
Color A – N 79 Tilleul
Color B – N 25 Aguamarina
Color C – N 30 Glicine
Color D – N 20 Jade

Block 2 – Make 8 Motifs
Color A – N 79 Tilleul
Color B – N 20 Jade
Color C – N 30 Glicine
Color D – N 20 Jade

Block 3 – Make 8 Motifs
Color A – N 79 Tilleul
Color B – N 54 Green Smoke
Color C – N 30 Glicine
Color D – N 20 Jade

First Motif (Block 1)

ROUNDS 1-5: Repeat Rounds 1-5 of Motif 9.

Motifs 2-26
Use photo and layout diagram as guide for color-way, Block placement and joining sides. Note: Remember to join the edge motifs and the bottom motifs to form the bag shape.

ROUNDS 1-4: Repeat Rounds 1-4 of Motif 9.
ROUND 5: Rep Round 5 of Motif 9, working the following across the side(s) for joining (from one corner to next corner):

Joining Side: (Start as established until corner for joining, then) 3-bob in next ch-3 sp, ch 1, working in previous motif, sl st in corresponding ch-3 sp, ch 1, working in current motif, 3-bob in same sp, [ch 2, dc in next ch-2 sp] 2 times, ch 2; 3-bob in next ch-3 sp, ch 1, working in previous motif, sl st in corresponding ch-3 sp, ch 1, working in current motif, 3-bob in same sp, (continue with [ch 2, dc in next sp], etc.)

Finishing
Using photo as guide, attach Straps to top of Bag.

Materials

Hook: E-4 (3.50 mm)

DMC Natura Just Cotton:
Colors:
Color A – N 87 Glacier
            N 80 Salomé
Color B – N 39 Ombre
            N 87 Glacier
Color C – N 80 Salomé

Finished Size: 4¾" x 74½"
(12 x 190 cm)

This project uses Motif 10 on page 40

PATTERN

Following instructions for Motif 10, and the join-as-you-go method on Round 4 (instructions below), use the following color-ways to make a total of 13 motifs. The layout for the Scarf is 1 motif wide and 13 motifs long, alternating Blocks.

Block 1 – Make 7 Motifs
Color A – N 87 Glacier
Color B – N 39 Ombre

Block 2 – Make 6 Motifs
Color A – N 80 Salomé
Color B – N 87 Glacier

First Motif (Block 1)

ROUNDS 1-4: Repeat Rounds 1-4 of Motif 10.

Motifs 2-13 (alternating Block 2 & Block 1)

ROUNDS 1-3: Repeat Rounds 1-3 of Motif 10.

ROUND 4: (Joining Round) Sl st in next ch-5 lp, ch 3, [yo, insert hook in same lp, pull up lp, yo, draw through 2 lps on hook] 2 times (3 lps on hook), yo and draw through all 3 lps (first 3-bob made), ch 5, 3-bob in same lp, ch 5, [sl st in center ch of next lp, ch 5] 4 times, (3-bob, ch 5, 3-bob) in next lp, ch 5, [sl st in center ch of next lp, ch 5] 4 times, holding previous motif behind current motif with right sides facing (wrong sides together), *in current motif, (3-bob, ch 2) in next lp, working in previous motif, sl st in corresponding center ch of corner ch-5 lp, ch 2, on current motif, 3-bob in same lp*, ch 2, on previous motif, sl st in center ch of next ch-5 lp, ch 2, [on current motif, sl st in center ch of next lp, ch 2, on previous motif, sl st in center ch of next lp, ch 2] 4 times; rep from * to * once, ch 5, [sl st in center ch of next lp, ch 5] 4 times; join with sl st to first dc (3rd ch of beg ch-3). Fasten off and weave in all ends.

SCARF BORDER: With right side facing, join Color C with sl st in any ch-5 lp, ch 1 (NOT counted as first st), (2 sc, ch 3, 2 sc) in same lp, ch 3, *(2 sc, ch 3, 2 sc) in next lp, ch 3; rep from * around; join with sl st to first sc. Fasten off and weave in all ends.

Doily

Materials

Hook: E-4 (3.50 mm)

DMC Natura Just Cotton:
Colors:
Color A – N 06 Rose Layette
Color B – N 44 Agatha

Finished Size: 14½" (37 cm) diameter

This project uses Motif 11 on page 42

PATTERN

Following instructions for Motif 11, and the join-as-you-go method on Round 5 (instructions below), make a total of 6 motifs.

First Motif

ROUNDS 1-5: Repeat Rounds 1-5 of Motif 11.

Motifs 2-5

ROUNDS 1-4: Repeat Rounds 1-4 of Motif 11.
ROUND 5: (One-Sided Joining) ♥[Ch 5, sl st in next ch-5 lp] 3 times, ch 5♥, (2 dc, ch 5, 2 dc) in next ch-5 lp, rep from ♥ to ♥ once, sl st in sp between next 2 sl sts; rep from ♥ to ♥ once, (2 dc, ch 2) in next ch-5 lp, working in previous motif, sl st in corner ch-5 lp, ch 2, on current motif, 2 dc in same lp; *[ch 2, on previous motif, sl st in next lp, ch 2, on current motif, sl st in next lp] 3 times, ch 2, on previous motif, sl st in next lp, ch 2, on current motif*, sl st in sp between next 2 sl sts; rep from * to * once, (2 dc, ch 2) in next ch-5 lp, working in previous motif, sl st in corner ch-5 lp, ch 2, on current motif, 2 dc in same lp; rep from ♥ to ♥ once, sl st in sp between next 2 sl sts. Fasten off Color B and weave in all ends.

Note: From Motif 3 onwards, make the join at the tip of triangle into the same center lps of previous motifs to form a circle.

Motif 6

ROUNDS 1-4: Repeat Rounds 1-4 of Motif 11.
ROUND 5: (Two-Sided Joining) ♥[Ch 5, sl st in next ch-5 lp] 3 times, ch 5♥, ♠(2 dc, ch 2) in next ch-5 lp, working in previous motif, sl st in corner ch-5 lp, ch 2, on current motif, 2 dc in same lp, *[ch 2, on previous motif, sl st in next lp, ch 2, on current motif, sl st in next lp] 3 times, ch 2, on previous motif, sl st in next lp, ch 2, on current motif*, sl st in sp between next 2 sl sts; rep from * to * once♠; rep from ♠ to ♠ once, (2 dc, ch 2) in next ch-5 lp, working in previous motif, sl st in corner ch-5 lp, ch 2, on current motif, 2 dc in same lp; rep from ♥ to ♥ once, sl st in sp between next 2 sl sts. Fasten off Color B and weave in all ends.

BORDER

ROUND 1: With right side facing, join Color B with sl st to 3rd ch of any ch-5 lp, ch 1 (NOT counted as first st, now and throughout), sc in same ch, *ch 5, sc in center ch of next ch-5 lp; rep from * around to last lp, ch 5, sc in center ch of last lp, ch 2; join with dc to first sc (to form last ch-5 lp and position yarn for next round).

ROUNDS 2-4: Ch 1, sc in lp under joining, *ch 5, sc in center ch of next ch-5 lp; rep from * around to last lp, ch 5, sc in center ch of last lp, ch 2; join with dc to first sc (to form last ch-5 lp and position yarn for next round).

ROUND 5: Ch 1, 3 sc in lp under joining, *(3 sc, ch 3, 3 sc) in next ch-5 lp; rep from * around, 3 sc in first lp, ch 3; join with sl st to first sc. Fasten off and weave in all ends.

Pastel Pillow

Materials

Hook: 3.5 mm

DMC Natura Just Cotton:
Colors:
Color A – N 43 Golden Lemon
Color B – N 82 Lobelia
        N 31 Malva
Color C – N 25 Aguamarina
Color D – N 76 Bamboo
Color E – N 30 Glicine
Color F – N 79 Tilleul
Color G – N 47 Safran

Fabric - for Pillow Back
Pillow Form

Finished Size: 15¾" x 15¾"
(40 x 40 cm)

This project uses Motif 12 on page 44

PATTERN

Following instructions for Motif 12, use the following color-ways to make a total of 36 motifs.

Block 1 – Make 18 Motifs
Color A – N 43 Golden Lemon
Color B – N 82 Lobelia
Color C – N 25 Aguamarina
Color D – N 76 Bamboo

Block 2 – Make 18 Motifs
Color A – N 43 Golden Lemon
Color B – N 31 Malva
Color C – N 25 Aguamarina
Color D – N 76 Bamboo

Assembly of Pillow Front
Use photo and layout diagram as guide.

With right sides facing, lay out all 36 motifs in a 6 x 6 square, alternating Blocks 1 & 2.

Motif Joining
Work across horizontal seams first.
♥Holding first two motifs together, with right sides facing (wrong sides together), working through both thicknesses, matching sts, working in back loops only, using Color E, join with sl st to corresponding chs of corner ch-1 sps, ch 1, sc in same ch, *sc in each st or ch across to ch of next corner**, pick up next two motifs and starting from corner ch of new motif, rep from * across seam, ending at ** on final repeat. Fasten off and weave in all ends.

Repeat from ♥ for the remaining horizontal seam.
Repeat from ♥ for both vertical seams.

Layout of Pillow Front

BORDER

ROUND 1: With right side facing, join Color F with sl st to any corner ch-1 sp, ch 1 (NOT counted as first st, now and throughout), (sc, ch 1, sc) in same corner, [sc in next st of sp] around, working (sc, ch 1, sc) in each corner; join with sl st to first sc. Fasten off Color F and weave in all ends.
ROUND 2: With right side facing, join Color G with sl st to any corner ch-1 sp, ch 1, *sc in each of next 3 sts (or sp), (sc, ch 3, sc) in next st or sp; rep from * around; join with sl st to first sc. Fasten off Color G and weave in all ends.

Finishing - use photo as guide
Sew Pillow Front to Fabric, making a pillow case and insert Pillow Form.

Sunshine Pillow

Materials

Hook: H-8 (5.00 mm)

DMC Natura XL:
Colors:
Color A – N 07 Sea Green
          N 81 Dark Blue
          N 82 Yellow
Color B – N 03 Off-White
Color C – N 73 Light Blue

Pillow Form

Finished Size: 16½" x 16½"
(42 x 42 cm)

This project uses Motif 13 on page 46

PATTERN

PILLOW FRONT

Following instructions for Motif 13, use the following color-ways to make a total of 16 motifs.

Block 1 – Make 4 Motifs
Color A – N 07 Sea Green
Color B – N 03 Off-White

Block 2 – Make 4 Motifs
Color A – N 81 Dark Blue
Color B – N 03 Off-White

Block 3 – Make 8 Motifs
Color A –N 82 Yellow
Color B – N 03 Off-White

Assembly of Pillow Front

Use photo and layout diagram as guide.

With right sides facing, lay out all 16 motifs in a 4 x 4 square, using rows of same color Blocks.

Motif Joining

Work across horizontal seams first.
♥Holding first two motifs together, with right sides facing (wrong sides together), working through both thicknesses, matching sts, working in back loops only, using Color C, join with sl st to corresponding chs of corner ch-1 sps, ch 1, sc in same ch, *sc in each st across to ch of next corner**, pick up next two motifs and starting from corner ch of new motif, rep from * across seam, ending at ** on final repeat. Fasten off and weave in all ends.

Repeat from ♥ for the remaining horizontal seam.
Repeat from ♥ for both vertical seams.

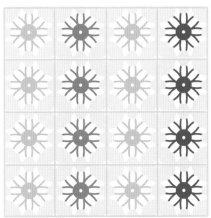

Layout of Pillow Front

At the end of the last seam, DO NOT FINISH OFF.

EDGING

ROUND 1: With right side facing, ch 1, working in back loops only, sc in each st or sp around; join with sl st to first sc.

PILLOW BACK

Base Row: Using Color B, ch 41.

ROW 1: (Right Side) Sc in 2nd ch from hook, [sc in next ch] across.
ROWS 2-41: Ch 1, turn, sc in each sc across.

At the end of Row 41, DO NOT FINISH OFF.

BORDER

ROUND 1: Ch 1, with wrong sides of Back and Front together and Front facing, working through both thicknesses and matching shaping, sc in each st around three sides, working (sc, ch 1, sc) in corner sps. insert Pillow Form and sc along last side; join with sl st to first sc. Fasten off and weave in all ends.

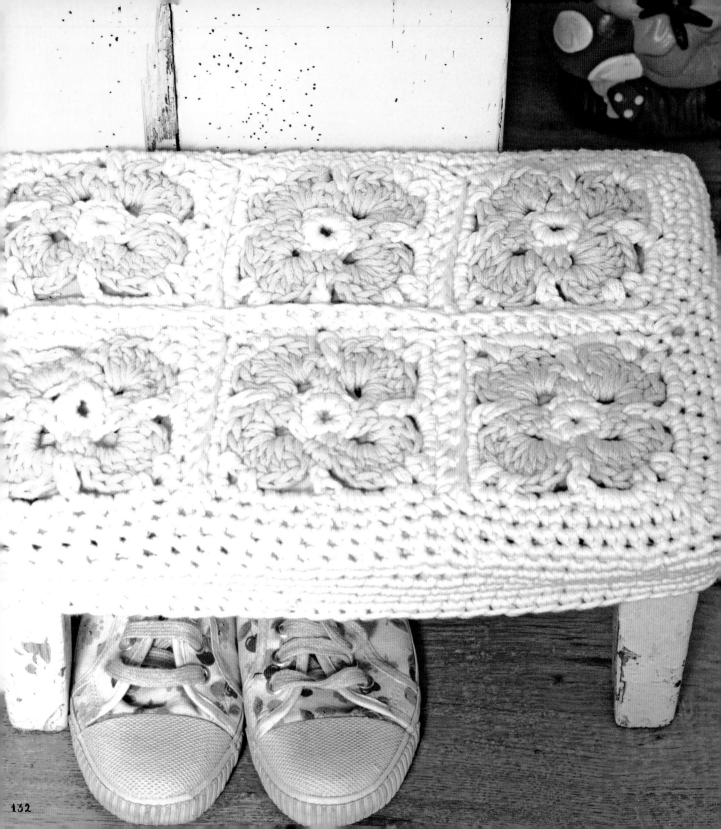

Foot Stool Cover

Materials

Hook: H-8 (5.00 mm)

DMC Natura XL:
Colors:
Color A – N 03 Off-White (2 balls)
Color B – N 73 Light Blue (1 ball)

Finished Size: 8½" x 11¾" (22 x 30 cm) top plus 2½" (6 cm) sides

This project uses Motif 20 on page 54

PATTERN

Following instructions for Motif 20, make a total of 6 motifs.

Assembly of Foot Stool Cover – use photo as guide

With right sides facing, lay out all 6 motifs – 3 across and 2 down.

Motif Joining
Work across horizontal seams first.
♥Holding first two motifs together, with right sides facing (wrong sides together), working through both thicknesses, matching sts, working in back loops only, using Color A, join with sl st to corresponding chs of corner ch-1 sps, ch 1, sc in same ch, *sc in each st across to ch of next corner**, pick up next two motifs and starting from corner ch of new motif, rep from * across seam, ending at ** on final repeat. Fasten off and weave in all ends.

Repeat from ♥ for the remaining horizontal seam.
Repeat from ♥ for both vertical seams.

At the end of the last seam, DO NOT FINISH OFF.

BORDER & SIDES

ROUND 1: With right side facing, ch 1, sc in same st, [sc in next st] around, working (sc, ch 1, sc) in each corner; join with sl st to first sc.

ROUNDS 2-4: Ch 1, sc in each sc around, working (sc, ch 1, sc) in each corner; join with sl st to first sc.

ROUNDS 5-10: Ch 1, sc in each st around; join with sl st to first sc.

At the end of Round 10, fasten off and weave in all ends.

Blanket

Materials

Hook: E-4 (3.50 mm)

DMC Natura Just Cottonn Colors:

Color A – N 06 Rose Layette
Color B – N 53 Blue Night
         N 32 Rose Saroya
Color C – N 13 Pistache
Color D – N 02 Ivory
Color E – N 25 Aguamarina
Color F – N 31 Malva
Color G – N 83 Blé

Finished Size: 31½" x 31½"
(80 x 80 cm)

This project uses Motif 33 on page 68

PATTERN

Following instructions for Rounds 1-3 of Motif 33 (fastening off at the end of Round 3), make a total of 36 motifs using the following color-ways:

Block 1 – Make 18 Motifs
Color A – N 06 Rose Layette
Color B – N 53 Blue Night
Color C – N 13 Pistache

Block 2 – Make 18 Motifs
Color A – N 06 Rose Layette
Color B – N 32 Rose Saroya
Color C – N 13 Pistache

With right sides facing, lay out motifs (using diagram as guide) - 6 motifs across and 6 motifs down – alternating color Blocks. Work the new Round 4 and the join-as-you-go method on Round 5 (instructions below) on all motifs.

All Motifs

ROUND 4: With right side facing, join Color D with sl st in any ch-6 lp, ch 1, 4 sc in same lp, ch 3, (3-bob, ch 5, 3-bob) in next ch-6 lp, ch 3, *4 sc in next lp, ch 3, (3-bob, ch 5, 3-bob) in next lp, ch 3; rep from * around; join with sl st to first sc. (8 bobbles, 16 sc, 8 ch-3 sps & 4 ch-5 lps) DO NOT FINISH OFF.

First Motif

ROUND 5: Ch 3, dc in each of next 3 sc, ch 1, 2 dc in next ch-3 sp, ch 1, (3 dc, ch 3, 3 dc) in next corner ch-5 lp, ch 1, 2 dc in next ch-3 sp, ch 1, *dc in each of next 4 sc, ch 1, 2 dc in next ch-3 sp, ch 1, (3 dc, ch 3, 3 dc) in next corner ch-5 lp, ch 1, 2 dc in next ch-3 sp, ch 1; rep from * around; join with sl st to first dc (3rd ch of beg ch-3). Fasten off and weave in all ends.

Motifs 2-36

Rep Round 5 of First Motif, working the following across the side(s) for joining (from one corner to next corner):

Joining Side: (Start as established until corner for joining, then:) 3 dc in next corner ch-5 lp, ch 1, working in previous motif, sl st in 3rd ch of corresponding ch-5 lp, ch 1, working in current motif, 3 dc in same lp,

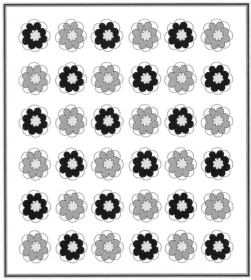

working in previous motif, sl st in next ch-1 sp, working in current motif, 2 dc in next ch-3 sp, working in previous motif, sl st in next ch-1 sp, working in current motif, dc in each of next 4 sc; rep from * to * once, 3 dc in next corner ch-5 lp, ch 1, working in previous motif, sl st in 3rd ch of corresponding ch-5 lp, ch 1, working in current motif, 3 dc in same lp, (continue with the next ch 1, 2 dc in next sp, etc.).

BORDER

ROUND 1: With right side facing, join Color D with sl st to any corner ch-3 sp, ch 6 (counts as first dc & ch-3), 3 dc in same sp, ch 2, [2 dc in next ch-2 sp, ch 2] across to next corner, *(3 dc, ch 3, 3 dc) in next corner ch-3 sp, ch 2, [2 dc, ch 2] in each ch-2 sp across to next corner; rep from * around, ending with 2 dc in first sp; join with sl st to first dc (3rd ch of beg ch-6).

ROUND 2: Sl st in next corner ch-3 sp, ch 3, (2 dc, ch 3, 3 dc) in same sp, ch 2, [2 dc, ch 2] in each ch-2 sp across to next corner, *(3 dc, ch 3, 3 dc) in next corner ch-3 sp, ch 2, [2 dc, ch 2] in each ch-2 sp across to next corner; rep from * around; join with sl st to first dc (3rd ch of beg ch-3). Fasten off Color D and weave in all ends.

ROUND 3: With right side facing, join Color E with sl st to any corner ch-3 sp, ch 1, (3 sc, ch 3, 3 sc) in same sp, ch 2, [2 sc in next ch-2 sp, ch 2] across to next corner, *(3 sc, ch 3, 3 sc) in next corner sp, ch 2, [2 sc in next ch-2 sp, ch 2] across to next corner; rep from * around; join with sl st to first sc. Fasten off Color E and weave in all ends.

ROUND 4: With right side facing, join Color F with sl st to any corner ch-3 sp, ch 1, (3 sc, ch 3, 3 sc) in same sp, ch 2, [2 sc in next ch-2 sp, ch 2] across to next corner, *(3 sc, ch 3, 3 sc) in next corner sp, ch 2, [2 sc in next ch-2 sp, ch 2] across to next corner; rep from * around; join with sl st to first sc. Fasten off Color F and weave in all ends.

ROUND 5: With right side facing, join Color G with sl st to any corner ch-3 sp, ch 1, (sc, ch 3, sc) in same sp, *(sc, ch 3, sc) in next sp; rep from * around; join with sl st to first sc. Fasten off Color G and weave in all ends.

Stitch Guide & Abbreviations

Slip Knot

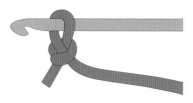

Create a loop with your yarn, making sure that the tail end is hanging behind your loop. Insert the hook through the loop, and pick up the ball end of the yarn.

Draw yarn through loop and pull on tail end gently to create slip knot on hook.

Chain

Nearly all crochet projects start with a series of chain stitches, as well as being used within stitch patterns. It is important to keep your tension even so the stitches are neither too tight nor too loose.

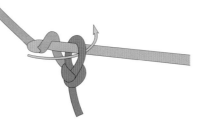

Start with a slip knot on your hook. Wrap yarn over hook and draw through loop on hook to complete chain stitch.

Single Crochet
(sc)

This is the shortest of the crochet stitches and one of the easiest and most commonly used stitches.

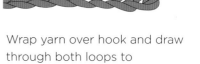

Start by inserting your hook into the indicated stitch or space. Wrap yarn over hook and draw through stitch or space. There are now 2 loops on the hook.

Wrap yarn over hook and draw through both loops to complete the stitch.

Double Crochet
(dc)

This stitch is the other most commonly used stitch. It is a taller stitch that creates a softer, more open fabric.

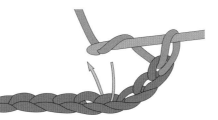

Start by wrapping yarn over hook once and then inserting hook into the indicated stitch or space. Wrap yarn over hook again and draw loop through. There are now 3 loops on the hook.

Wrap yarn over hook again and draw through both loops to complete the stitch.

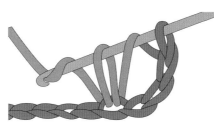

Wrap yarn over hook and draw through first 2 loops.

Half Double Crochet
(hdc)

This stitch is halfway in height between a single crochet and double crochet.

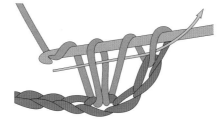

Start by wrapping yarn over hook once and then inserting hook into the indicated stitch or space. Wrap yarn over hook again and draw loop through. There are nor 3 loops on the hook. Wrap yarn over hook and draw through all 3 loops to complete the stitch.

Treble (or Triple) Crochet (tr)

This stitch is taller than double crochet and is often used in decorative stich patterns or to add height to corners.

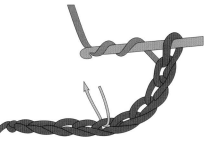

Start by wrapping yarn over hook twice and then inserting hook into the indicated stitch or space.

Wrap yarn over hook and draw loop through. There are now 4 loops on the hook.

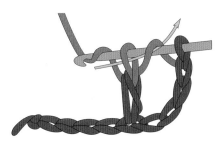

Wrap yarn over hook and draw through first 2 loops. There are now 3 loops on the hook. Wrap yarn over hook and draw through 2 loops on hook. There are now 2 loops on the hook.

Wrap yarn over and draw through remaining 2 loops to complete the stitch.

Double Treble (dtr)
Triple Treble (ttr)

These stitches are worked in the same way as a treble stitch. The stitch height is altered by the amount of times you wrap the yarn around your hook at the beginning of the stitch.

A double treble is started by wrapping yarn over hook 3 times.

A triple treble is started by wrapping yarn over hook 4 times.

The stitch is then completed in the same way as a treble by wrapping yarn over hook and drawing through 2 loops at a time until the end.

Slip Stitch (sl st)

This stitch does not add height to your work and is most commonly used to move to a different position or for joining.

To start, insert the hook into the indicated stitch or space. Yarn over hook and draw through stitch or space and the loop on hook.

Shells

This stitch is most often used as a decorative scalloped border and is generally made using taller stitches such as double or treble crochet.

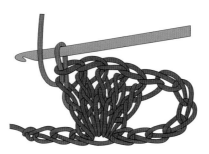

Shells are formed by working a number of stitches into the same point.

To make a shell, work the specified number of stitches into the same space.

Clusters (cl)

Clusters are the reverse of a shell in that a number of stitches are worked before joining together at the top. This creates a shell that fans out downwards.

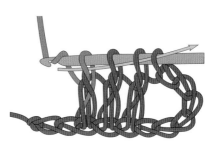

To make a double crochet cluster, work the stitch as normal but stopping at the final step of drawing yarn through last 2 loops. Keep these loops on hook and make a double crochet in the next stitch, but stopping before the final step. Continue working this way for the required amount of stitches.

Once you have all your stitches made, yarn over hook and draw through all loops to complete cluster.

Bobbles

Bobbles are a textural stitch, giving your work a raised surface. They are worked in a similar way to a cluster except that all the stitches are worked into the same space.

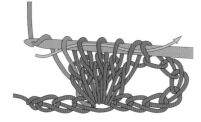

Work your stitches as normal but stop at the final step of drawing yarn through last 2 loops. Keep these loops on your hook and start the next double crochet, into the same stitch but stopping before the final step. Continue working this way until the required amount of stitches have been made.
Normally a bobble will be secured at the top by a chain stitch. However some patterns may specify not to complete this step. Always check the pattern whether this step in required.

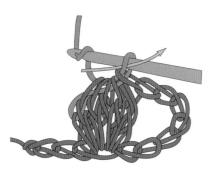

Puff Stitches

A puff stitch is similar to a bobble stitch but is made using half double crochet stitches and is smoother and plumper than a bobble.

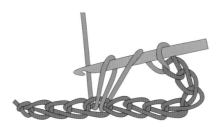

Start by making an incomplete half double crochet stitch (i.e. don't complete the final stage of drawing yarn through last 3 loops. When starting each new half double crochet, draw the loop up higher than normal.

Once the required number of stitches have been made, draw yarn through all loops on hook.

Normally this stitch will be secured by a chain stitch. However this will vary according to the pattern. Check the pattern instructions first.

Popcorns

This stitch is similar to a shell but it is drawn together at the top to create surface texture.

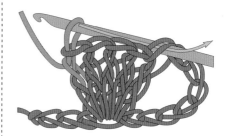

Work the required number of stitches into the same space. When the last stitch has been completed, remove hook and insert into the top of the first stitch of the group, pick up dropped loop.

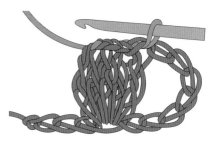

Yarn over hook, draw through both loops to complete.

The completed popcorn will sit away from the surface of your work.

Abbreviations

[ ]	Work instructions within brackets as many times as directed.					
( )	Work instructions within parentheses in same stitch or space indicated.					
*****	Repeat the instructions following the single asterisk as directed.					
******	1) Repeat instructions between asterisks as many times as directed; or 2) Repeat from a given set of instructions.					
"	inch(es)	**dtr**	double treble	**rep(s)**	repeat(s)
beg	begin/beginning	**g**	gram	**rnd(s)**	round(s)
ch(s)	chain(s)	**hdc**	half-double crochet	**sc**	single crochet
ch-	chain previously made	**inc**	increase	**sl st(s)**	slip stich(es)
ch-sp	chain space	**lp(s)**	loop(s)	**sp(s)**	space(s)
ch-st	chain stitch	**m**	meter(s)	**st(s)**	stitch(es)
cl	cluster	**mm**	millimeter	**tog**	together
cm(s)	centimeter(s)	**oz(s)**	ounce(s)	**tr**	treble crochet
dc	double crochet	**pc**	popcorn	**yd(s)**	yard(s)
dec	decrease	**rem**	remaining	**yo**	yarn over

DMC NATURA XL COLOR PALETTE

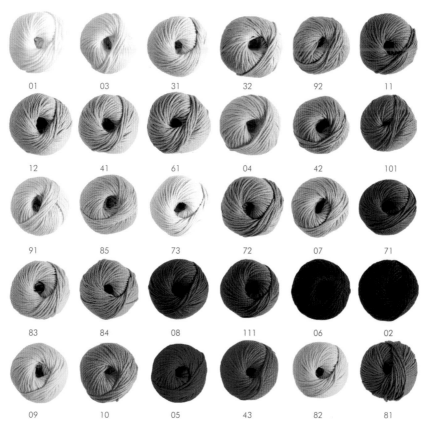

01	03	31	32	92	11
12	41	61	04	42	101
91	85	73	72	07	71
83	84	08	111	06	02
09	10	05	43	82	81

Natura
Just Cotton

DMC NATURA COLOR PALETTE

In this book we use DMC Natura Just Cotton,
here you can see the compelete range of 60 colours.

N 01	Ibiza	N 26	Blue Jeans	N 30	Glicine
N 02	Ivory	N 28	Zaphire	N 88	Orléans
N 35	Nacar	N 27	Star Light	N 31	Malva
N 36	Gardenia	N 53	Blue Night	N 59	Prune
N 37	Canelle	N 49	Turquoise	N 45	Orquidea
N 78	Lin	N 64	Prussian	N 44	Agatha
N 39	Ombre	N 54	Green Smoke	N 80	Salomé
N 22	Tropic Brown	N 14	Green Valley	N 03	Sable
N 41	Siena	N 46	Forêt	N 83	Blé
N 86	Brique	N 38	Liquen	N 16	Tournesol
N 85	Giroflée	N 81	Acanthe	N 75	Moss Green
N 47	Safran	N 82	Lobelia	N 43	Golden Lemon
N 18	Coral	N 52	Geranium	N 74	Curry
N 23	Passion	N 07	Spring Rose	N 12	Light Green
N 34	Bourgogne	N 06	Rose Layette	N 79	Tilleul
N 87	Glacier	N 32	Rose Soraya	N 76	Bamboo
N 20	Jade	N 51	Erica	N 13	Pistache
N 25	Aguamarina	N 33	Amaranto	N 48	Chartreuse
N 05	Bleu Layette	N 62	Cerise	N 09	Gris Argent
N 56	Azur	N 61	Crimson	N 11	Noir